THE WAY OF ST JAMES
(Camino de Santiago)

PYRENEES–SANTIAGO–FINISTERRE
A Walker's Guide

D0019273

ABOUT THE AUTHOR

Alison Raju is a former teacher of French, German and Spanish to adults and the author of several other guides to pilgrimage routes published by Cicerone Press: *The Pilgrim Road to Nidaros: St Olav's Way Oslo to Trondheim*, *The Way of St James: Via de la Plata: Seville to Santiago*, as well as earlier editions of this guide: *The Way of St James: Le Puy to Santiago*.

THE WAY OF ST JAMES

(Camino de Santiago)

PYRENEES–SANTIAGO–FINISTERRE
A Walker's Guide

by
Alison Raju

2 POLICE SQUARE, MILNTHORPE, CUMBRIA LA7 7PY
www.cicerone.co.uk

© Alison Raju, 2003

ISBN-10 1-85284-372-1
ISBN-13 978-1-85284-372-4

Reprinted 2005

A catalogue record for this book is available from the British Library.

Photos by the author, except where otherwise credited.
Maps drawn by Harvey Map Services.

Dedication
For all those who begin their journey as a
long-distance walk and end it as a pilgrimage

Acknowledgements
I would like to thank Marigold Fox for
her assistance in compiling Appendix B

Advice to Readers

Readers are advised that while every effort is taken by the author to ensure the accuracy of this guidebook, changes can occur which may affect the contents. It is advisable to check locally on transport, accommodation, shops, etc, but even rights of way can be altered.

The publisher would welcome notes of any such changes.

Front cover: Santiago Cathedral (Photo: Ysabel Halpin)

CONTENTS

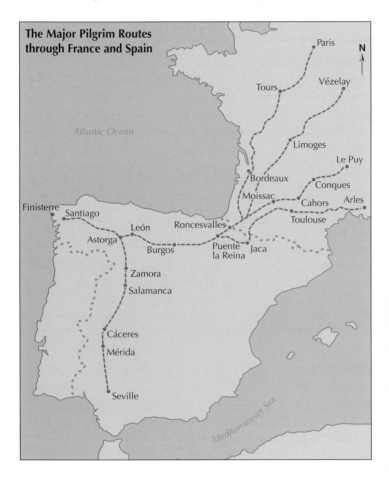

The Major Pilgrim Routes through France and Spain

N

Paris

Vézelay

Tours

Atlantic Ocean

Limoges

Le Puy

Bordeaux

Conques

Moissac

Cahors

Arles

Toulouse

Finisterre

Santiago

León

Roncesvalles

Astorga

Burgos

Puente la Reina

Jaca

Zamora

Salamanca

Cáceres

Mérida

Seville

Mediterranean Sea

INTRODUCTION

The Way of St James as described in this book is a long-distance footpath with a difference. People have been walking it – as a pilgrimage route – for over a thousand years, and in 1987 the section from the Spanish monastery at Roncesvalles in the foothills of the Pyrenees to Santiago de Compostela became the first European Cultural Itinerary. The 800km route, running across northern Spain to the City of the Apostle in the western reaches of Galicia, has changed little in all that time. For although parts of it have now become modern tarred roads, and many of its 'hospitals' and other accommodation set up by religious orders along the way to minister to the needs of pilgrims have long since disappeared, the *Camino de Santiago*, as it is known in Spain, still passes through the same villages, climbs the same hills, crosses the same rivers and visits the same chapels, churches, cathedrals and other monuments as did the route taken by our predecessors in centuries gone by.

The Way of St James is also a long-distance footpath with a difference in that many of those who walk the route through France and the vast majority of those who start on the Spanish side of the Pyrenees are not experienced walkers. Many have never done any serious walking in their lives and many will never do any

again; for here, as in the past, walking is a means of transport, a means to an end, rather than an activity for its own sake. Most long-distance footpaths also avoid not only large towns but also even quite small villages; the Way of St James, on the other hand, because of its historic origins and the need for shelter, deliberately seeks them out. Several thousand people walk the Way every year, whether from points on the *camino* in Spain, from the Pyrenees, from different parts of France, or from even further afield: it is not uncommon, even nowadays, to meet Swiss, German, Belgian or Dutch pilgrims, for example, who have set out from home to make the entire journey on foot. However, one of the differences between the modern pilgrim and his historical counterpart, whether he walks, goes by bicycle or on horseback, is that very few return home by the same means of transport. The modern pilgrim route has thus become a 'one-way street' and it is unusual, today, to encounter anyone with either enough time or the inclination to return to their point of departure by the same means as used on their outward journey.

People make the journey to Santiago for a variety of reasons – historical, cultural, religious, as a significant action or event in their lives – and it is something that many

Family on the camino
(Photo: Paddy Dillon)

Spaniards in particular think of doing at least once in their lifetime, even if they do not actually manage to. Twenty-first-century pilgrims are people of all ages and from all walks of life, the majority from Spain, but with a great many each year from France, Switzerland, Belgium, Holland and Germany, and others from much further away. (In contrast there are relatively few from Britain at present.) Many travel alone, many in twos and threes, many in quite large groups, particularly those on foot. Many complete the entire journey in one stretch; others, with more limited time, walk only from León, Astorga or O Cebreiro, for example, or cover a section at a time over several years. Most who walk the Way of St James, and especially those who have been able to do the whole route in one go, would probably agree afterwards that it has changed their lives in some way, even though they may not have set out with this intention.

This book replaces the second part of the present author's previous one-volume guide published by Cicerone Press: *The Way of St James: Le Puy to Santiago* (1999). The Way described in this book thus begins in Saint-Jean-Pied-de-Port, as those who wish to walk only the Spanish section will find it more convenient to start from there than from Roncesvalles, despite having a stiff climb on their first day. It is easier to reach the former by public transport (Paris–Bayonne–Saint-Jean) than by going to

Madrid, Bilbao or Irún and then back-tracking to the latter. From the border town on the French side of the Pyrenees the route crosses over into Spain and wends its way through Navarra, Castilla y León and Galicia to Santiago de Compostela. Likewise, for those who feel that their pilgrimage would be incomplete unless they continued on to Finisterre on foot a description of this route is given at the end of this volume. Appendices contain an outline guide to the *Camino aragonès* from the Spanish border to Puenta la Reina, a summary of St James's and other pilgrim references along the route through Spain, a glossary of geographical and other frequently encountered terms, and a list of suggestions for further reading.

The walk from the Pyrenees to Santiago can be completed in four to five weeks by anyone who is fairly fit and who also likes to visit places of interest along the way. It can be undertaken in sections, too, by those who lack the time to do it all in one go or who would just like to cover certain stretches, and indications are given in the text as to how to reach (or leave) the main towns along the Way. Anyone in Britain who is thinking of walking, cycling or riding any part of the route should certainly consider contacting the Confraternity of St James for advice and membership: their annually updated guide to accommodation and facilities on the route is extremely useful (see Appendix D for the address). The

9

walker's route is not normally suitable for cyclists, even those on mountain bikes, and anyone wishing to cycle by road should obtain John Higginson's *Way of St James: Le Puy to Santiago – A Cyclist's Guide* (1999), also published by Cicerone Press.

HISTORY

Pilgrims have been travelling to Santiago de Compostela on foot or on horseback (and more recently by bicycle) for over a thousand years. Godescalc, Bishop of Le Puy, who went there in AD951, was one of the first. At the height of its popularity in the 11th and 12th centuries over half a million people are said to have made the pilgrimage from different parts of Europe each year, the majority of them from France.

Pilgrimages had been popular amongst Christians ever since Constantine the Great had the Church of the Holy Sepulchre built over the site of Christ's burial in Jerusalem in AD326, and the discovery, shortly afterwards, of the Holy Cross itself. Those journeying to this shrine were known as *palmeros* (palmers). *Romeros* went to Rome, the burial place of St Peter, the other great centre of Christian pilgrimage in the Middle Ages, along with Santiago de Compostela after the finding of the remains of St James the Great (son of Zebedee, brother of John and Christ's cousin). The high point of this third pilgrimage

10

occurred between the years AD1000 and 1500. But although numbers dwindled after that due to the Reformation and other, political, factors, the stream of pilgrims making the trudge westwards from different parts of Europe to the far reaches of Galicia in northwest Spain never completely dried up, and since the late 20th century has been making something of a comeback. The Cathedral authorities in Santiago maintain a register of pilgrims, and in 1991 recorded a total of 7274 travelling on foot, bicycle or horseback (compared with 5760 in 1989, the year of the Pope's August visit), and 4918 in 1990. In the 1993 Holy Year (a year in which St James's Day, 25 July, falls on a Sunday, and in which special dispensations are available – see below), a record 99,436 pilgrims received their *compostelas* (certificate of pilgrimage) though not all, by any means, began in Roncesvalles, let alone further afield. The numbers fell, predictably, in 1994 (15,863), though they began to rise again in 1995 (19,821), 1996 (23,218), 1997 (25,179) and 1998 (30,126), to reach a staggering 155,000 in the 1999 Holy Year. In 2000 (a jubilee year because of the Millennium) there were 55,004 pilgrims, in 2001 61,418, and in 2002 65,000.

Legend

Pilgrims who have walked from Le Puy-en-Velay using the companion volume to this guide will already

*Church of Santiago el Real with
equestrian statue of Santiago
Matamoros, Logroño*

know that after the death of Christ the disciples dispersed to different parts of the then known world, to spread the Gospel as they had been bidden. Little is known about the life of St James, but he went to Spain, where he spent a couple of years evangelising, though apparently without a great deal of success. He returned to Jerusalem but was beheaded by Herod shortly afterwards, in AD44. Immediately following his martyrdom, his followers are said to have taken his body to Jaffa, on the coast, where a ship was miraculously waiting for them and they set off back to Spain. They landed in Iria Flavia on the coast of Galicia, present-day Padrón, some 20km from what is now Santiago de Compostela, after a journey (and in a *stone* boat!) which is purported to have taken only a week, thereby providing proof of angelic assistance. The body was buried in a tomb on a hillside, along with two of his followers later on, and forgotten for the next 750 years.

Early in the 9th century Pelagius, a hermit living in that part of Spain, had a vision (which he subsequently reported to Theodomir, bishop of Ira Flavia) in which he saw a very large bright star, surrounded by a ring of smaller ones, shining over a deserted spot in the hills. The matter was investigated and a tomb containing three bodies was found there, immediately identified as those of St James and two of his followers. When Alfonso II, King of the Asturias (791–824), went

there he declared St James the patron saint of Spain. He built a church and a small monastery over the tomb in the saint's honour, around which a town grew up. It was known as *campus de la stella* or *campus stellae*, later shortened to *compostela* – one explanation of the origin of the name. Another is that it derives from the Latin *componere* (to bury), as a Roman cemetery or early Christian necropolis is known to have existed under the site of the present-day Cathedral in Santiago – and where the remains of St James are still believed to be housed today.

The Pilgrimage

News of the discovery soon spread. It was encouraged to do so, both by Archbishop Gelmírez and the Cathedral authorities (anxious to promote the town as a pilgrimage centre, thus attracting money to the area), and by the monks of Cluny (who saw in it the opportunity to assist the Spanish church in their long struggle against the Moors). Both factions were also helped by the fact that the Turks had seized the Holy Sepulchre in 1078, thus putting a stop to pilgrimages to Jerusalem. However, Santiago was attractive as a potential pilgrim 'venue' in other respects too, as it fulfilled the various criteria necessary to make a pilgrimage there worthy of merit. It was far away (from most parts of France, for example) and difficult to reach, thus requiring a good deal of hardship and endurance

Modern fresco in the fine Benedictine monastery in the village of Samos
(Photo: Paddy Dillon)

to get there (and back again). It was sufficiently dangerous (wolves, bandits, fever, rivers that were difficult to cross, unscrupulous ferrymen) as well as being in Spain, then locked tight in struggle with the Moors, and for this reason many pilgrims travelled in quite large groups. (A considerable corpus of pilgrim songs from previous centuries still exists, sung by the pilgrims as they walked.)

The road itself was also well supplied with shrines, relics and other sights worth seeing. As traffic increased roads, bridges and hospices were built. The pilgrimage churches, characterised by ambulatories round the inside of the building in order to facilitate viewing of the relics exposed behind the high altar, were endowed with a growing number of such items,

thus ensuring that pilgrims would pass that way to see them. Many churches were dedicated to St James and many more contain his statue, whether as *Santiago apóstol*, as a pilgrim (*Santiago peregrino*) or as the Moor-slayer *(Santiago matamoros)*. He is the subject of paintings and stained glass too – with a halo as St James the Apostle; without when he is portrayed as a pilgrim. A considerable number of very tiny chapels or *ermitas* dedicated to St Roch (San Roque in Spanish), the pilgrim saint from Montpellier, were also built along the way. After a pilgrimage to Rome St Roch devoted his life to caring for plague victims, but withdrew to live in a forest when he contracted a disease which left him with an unsightly sore on his left thigh. (For this reason he is

13

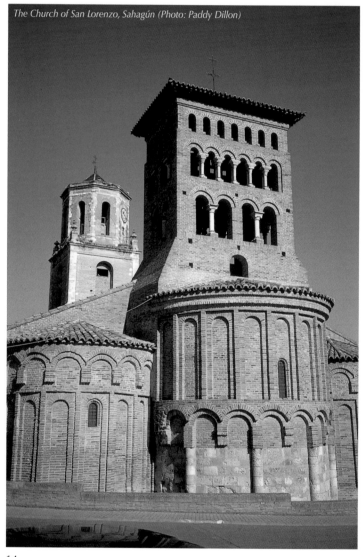

The Church of San Lorenzo, Sahagún (Photo: Paddy Dillon)

depicted in art with the front flap of his coat turned back, to warn people to keep away from him, and is accompanied by the faithful dog – often with a loaf of bread in his mouth – who brought the saint his daily rations. Legend has confused him with *Santiago peregrino* at times, and he not infrequently appears in a 'pilgrim version' as well, with hat, staff and scallop shells on his clothing.)

So why did people go on pilgrimages? For a variety of reasons: as a profession of faith, as a form of punishment (a system of fixed penalties for certain crimes/sins was in operation during the Middle Ages), as a means of atonement, as a way of acquiring merit (and thus, for example, reducing or, in certain cases, cutting in half, the amount of time spent in Purgatory) and as an opportunity to venerate the relics of the many saints available along the principal routes to Santiago. (Indulgences were available to those who visited shrines.) No doubt, too, there were some who were just glad of the opportunity to escape their surroundings. Later there were professional pilgrims who would (for a fee) undertake the pilgrimage on behalf of someone else who could afford the money but not the time to do it him or herself. Those with the means to do so went on horseback, and some wealthy people made the pilgrimage along with a considerable retinue. The majority of pilgrims went on foot, however, and even amongst the rich there were some who preferred to walk, rather than ride, because of the greater 'merit' they would attain.

The pilgrim in former times was not at all sure that he would reach his destination, let alone return home in one piece, so before setting out he took leave of his family and employer, made his will and generally put his affairs in order. He (or she) obtained his credentials (pilgrim passport) from his bishop or church, which he could then present in order to obtain food and lodging in the many pilgrim 'hospitals' and other establishments along the way. This was both a precaution against the growing number of *coquillards* (pseudo-pilgrims) and a means of providing proof of his journey: he had his papers stamped at different stages along the way so that once he arrived in Santiago he could obtain his *compostela* or certificate of pilgrimage from the Cathedral authorities. This in turn entitled him to stay in the pilgrim shelters on his return journey as well as furnishing evidence, if needed, that he had actually made the pilgrimage successfully.

The pilgrim had his staff and scrip (knapsack) blessed in church before setting out and travelled light, carrying little else but a gourd for water. The scallop shell – the *concha* or *coquille Saint-Jacques* – which has for many people become an essential ingredient of 'pilgrim uniform' was, in former times, something that was carried *back* from Santiago by the returning pilgrim; these were found on the

Galician coast and served as additional proof that the pilgrim had reached his destination. It was also the symbol embedded above doorways and elsewhere on the many and varied buildings that accommodated pilgrims along the different roads to Santiago.

Pilgrims with funds could obviously stay in inns and other publicly available lodgings, but the vast majority probably stayed in the different hospices and other facilities specially provided for them. Some of these were in towns (either in the centre, or outside the walls to cater both for latecomers and possibly contagious pilgrims). Others were in the countryside, often by bridges or at the crossing of important pilgrims' feeder roads. Much of the pilgrim accommodation was provided by religious orders such as the Benedictines and the Antonins, by churches and civic authorities, as well as by benevolent individuals. The facilities offered varied considerably from one establishment to another and records survive from many, indicating exactly what was provided for the pilgrim.

There are different explanations as to the origins of the *concha* or *coquille Saint-Jacques*, but one is that when the followers of St James arrived in the port of Iria Flavia with the apostle's body they saw a man riding along the beach (a bridegroom in some versions). His horse took fright and plunged into the sea. When the pair re-emerged both horse and rider were covered from head to

foot in scallop shells (even today the beaches in this part of Galicia are strewn with them). It was customary to set out in the springtime in order to reach Santiago for the feast of St James on 25 July and return home for the winter. This was especially true in Holy Years, when 25 July falls on a Sunday (the next ones are in 2004, 2010, 2021, 2027 and 2032 – a pattern of 6–11–6–5 years), the only time the *Puerta Santa* or Holy Door of the Cathedral of Santiago is open. This is sealed up at the end of each such year and then symbolically broken down again by the Archbishop in a special ceremony in the evening of 31 December preceding the new Holy Year, a year during which special concessions and indulgences were, and still are, available to pilgrims. On returning home many joined confraternities of former pilgrims in their own countries, the forerunners of the modern-day associations of 'Friends of St James' that now exist in several countries to support, promote and encourage the different routes to Santiago.

Many pilgrims wrote accounts of their experiences, but as early as the 12th century the first real 'travel guide' was produced, probably between 1140–50. Its author was for a long time believed to be one Aimery Picaud, a cleric from Parthenay-le-Vieux in the Poitou region of France, and it formed part of a Latin manuscript known as the *Codex Calixtinus*. However, instead of relating the journey of one particular individual this was intended as a guide for the use of prospective (especially French) pilgrims. It describes the four most important roads through France and divides the route from the Pyrenees to Santiago into 13 (somewhat unequal) stages. It lists, with comments, the places through which the *Camino francés* (see below) passes, indicates some of the hazards pilgrims may encounter, and contains advice on the rivers along the way, indicating which are safe to drink from and which should be avoided.

The author also describes in some detail the inhabitants of the different regions through which the prospective pilgrim will pass, their language (including one of the earliest lists of Basque words), customs and characteristics, none of which compare at all favourably, in his opinion, with those of the people of his native Poitou. He includes a list of shrines to be visited along the different roads through France, a description of the city of Santiago and its churches, and a detailed account of the Cathedral's history, architecture and canons.

It is now thought that this guide was not written by one person but was a compilation, designed (under the influence of the energetic bishop Diego Gelmírez) to promote Santiago de Compostela as a pilgrimage centre. Regardless of its authorship, this guide was certainly instrumental in popularising the itineraries of the four main pilgrim roads through France and the *Camino francés* in Spain. It has recently been translated into English (see Appendix C).

Routes to Santiago

The route described in this book is not, in fact, the one and only 'Way of St James'. In former times, when pilgrims set out from their own front doors and made their way to Santiago from many different places, several well-established routes grew up (see map, page 6). In France, for example, there were four main departure points, each with several 'feeder roads' joining them at different points along the way, and a whole network of pilgrim routes from 'farther back' in Germany, Austria, Switzerland, Belgium, Holland and beyond. The route from Paris, the *Via Turonensis*, the *Via Lemovicensis* starting in Vézélay and the *Via Podensis* from Le Puy-en-Velay all joined up near Ostabat on the French side of the Pyrenees, to continue over the mountains to Roncesvalles and on across the north of Spain as the *Camino francés* or 'French road'. The fourth way, from Arles, and known as the *Via Tolosana*, crossed the Pyrenees further east at the Col de Somport, from where it is known as the *Camino aragonés* (see Appendix A), before merging with the other three at Puenta la Reina.

Although the name *Camino de Santiago* has become synonymous with the *Camino francés* in Spain, other important routes included the northern one along the Costa Cantabrica, passing through Hernani, Zumaya, Guernica, Bilbao, Lareda and Casteñada before turning inland to reach Santiago via Oviedo and Lugo. This was the path taken by many English pilgrims, who went by ship as far as Bordeaux and then continued on foot, whilst others sailed to La Coruña and then walked the rest of the way along one of the *Rutas del Mar*, one of which was known as the *Camino inglés*. The *Vía de la Plata* or *Camino mozárabe*, on the other hand, was the way taken by pilgrims from the south of Spain and others joining it by sea in Seville, passing through Mérida, Cáceres, Salamanca and Zamora before either joining the *Camino francés* in Astorga or continuing directly to Santiago via Puebla de Sanabria and Ourense along the *Camino de Santiago meridional*. There were also routes from the east coast of Spain as well as two *caminos*, south to north, through Portugal, one inland, the other along the coast. The 'Way of St James' described here therefore corresponds to the one known as the *Camino francés*, nowadays the most widely used and best-documented of the many pilgrim roads to Santiago. It begins in this book in Saint-Jean-Pied-de-Port, on the French side of the Pyrenees, and passes through Roncesvalles, Pamplona, Estella, Logroño, Burgos, Sahagún, León, Astorga, Ponferrada,

Villafranca del Bierzo and Sarria. It is also known that many pilgrims in former times continued their journey beyond Santiago to what was then the end of the known world in Finisterre, a walkers' route described as an integral part of this volume.

TOPOGRAPHY, ECONOMY AND LANGUAGE

The Way of St James through Spain begins in the Basque country. This is a geographical entity which (as opposed to the present-day Spanish autonomous *región* of the *País vasco*) flanks both sides of the Pyrenees, three of its provinces in France (Laborde, Basse-Navarre and Soule), the other four in Spain (Alava, Guipúzcoa, Navarra and Viscaya). Pilgrims who have walked through France will notice features already encountered on the other side of the Pyrenees: place names in both languages (Basque and French or Castilian), for example, and a distinctive local architecture. In both countries the large Basque houses with their overhanging eaves, often ornately decorated, outside staircases and balconies running the whole length of one or more sides of the building are common, as is the *frontón* or pelota court, to be found in almost every village of any size. The Basque language (*Euskerra* in Basque, *Vascuence* in Castilian) is unrelated to any of the Romance languages and its origins are still the subject of scholarly debate. It is an official language in the four

Crossing the Pyrenees (Photo: Paddy Dillon)

Alferero (potter) sculpture, Navarrete

Basque provinces in Spain, alongside Castilian, and is much in evidence in Navarre, whether in ordinary conversation, on television (in bars, for example), on signs and notices or on place-name boards.

After the high mountains and deep valleys of the Pyrenees, where sheep are a common sight, the landscape changes, flattening out to become more undulating as the *camino* makes its way down to Pamplona, a fortress town set on a hill in the middle of a wide, fertile plain. It also gets hotter and dustier in summer, when it rarely rains, and the older vernacular houses are brown, built in adobe with red pantile roofs. This area has much in common with the landscape of Castille-León, though you remain in Navarre until the outskirts of Logroño.

La Rioja, like Navarre, is both a province and an autonomous *región* (Spain is divided into 17 of the latter, each containing one or several *provincias*) and is well known for its excellent wines. It is also characterised by a deep-red clay soil, contrasting sharply with the golden summer corn, the bright blue of the sky and the dark green of the many trees, particularly in the early morning and evening light. You will come across a number of potteries or *alfarerías*, especially in the section between Logroño and Nájera. From here to Burgos (before it climbs up into the woods in the Montes de Oca) the *camino* continues through undulating countryside where you will encounter – as in many other parts of Spain – large flocks of sheep and goats, often on the move with their shepherds and goatherds, in search of new grazing on cornfields that have just been harvested.

As you continue into Castille-León, one of the largest of the autonomous regions (with nine provinces), you will meet the first of a special type of local inhabitant: the *cigüeña*. The ubiquitous stork has a nest (and sometimes as many as three or four) on the tower of nearly every church and is a characteristic sight in this part of Spain, as are the seemingly endless cornfields. After Burgos the *camino* wends its way up onto the *meseta*, the high plateau or tableland where the walker often has the feeling of being on the 'roof of the world'. After this it descends through the rolling countryside of the province of Palencia into the flat plains of León where several place names include the suffix *del Páramo* (bleak plateau/plain). (Other places along the Way of St James in Spain end in *del Camino*, evidence of the route the pilgrims took in former times.)

After Astorga the *camino* enters the Montes de León, slowly, at first, through the area known as the Maragatería. There are different theories as to the origins of the people here, with their distinctive customs, traditions and music. One suggests that, because of their isolated situation, they are the descendants of a very ancient race who escaped the

Camino before a storm (Photo: Ysabel Halpin)

effects of successive invasions. There are many abandoned or semi-abandoned villages amongst the 45 that make up the Maragatería, some of which are now coming to life again, largely due to the revival of interest in the *Camino de Santiago*. An example of a typical *maragato* village, now a National Monument and worth a short detour, is Castrillo de los Polvares, just off the route beyond Astorga. Pilgrims interested in gastronomy may wish to try the *cocido maragato* while they are in this area, an *extremely* substantial preparation in four parts: a large plateful of stew, made of six or seven different types of meat, followed by an equally large plateful of chick peas and cooked green vegetables, a (large, again!) plateful of soup and a somewhat smaller dish, of either rice pudding or *natillas* (a type of custard), to finish. (It will be obvious that a lengthy siesta needs to be built into your schedule after one of these meals...)

After the Cruz de Fierro, the highest point on the route (1504m), the *camino* enters the mountainous area of El Bierzo, sometimes thought of as Galicia's fifth province, with its fertile valleys and excellent wines, though the latter are not yet as internationally well known as those of La Rioja. Then after Vega de Valcarce (still in the province of León but totally different from the landscape where the *camino* enters it 7km before Sahagún) the pilgrim road climbs up and up, through chestnut woods, and then out into open country up to the tiny village of O Cebreiro (1300m),

Spring emerging from the ground (Photo: Ysabel Halpin)

shortly before which it enters Galicia. From here the route changes dramatically in character.

Galicia is the autonomous *región* comprising the provinces of Lugo, Ourense, Pontevedra and La Coruña. It has its own language, related to Portuguese, and which, together with *castellano* ('Spanish') is used as the official language in the region. As a result you will not only find that people will reply to you in *gallego* but that all road signs, official notices and so on appear in both languages. The spelling of place names often varies between the two languages, and as at present the *castellano* forms have not yet been officially standardised the names on maps and notices may differ from what you see on signposts and on entry to vil-

lages big enough to have place-name boards. If versions given in this guide appear inconsistent at times it is because they are based on those seen on street and place-name boards and signposts along the way, not on those found on maps and/or in other guidebooks (and so the Galician term is often the one given). Some of the more common spelling variations are the interchange of 'b' and 'v' (as in Valos/Balos, for example), 'o' and 'ou' and 'e' and 'ei'.

Galicia is a very green, lush area for the most part, with the highest rainfall in Spain. Unlike the south of Spain with its enormous *latifundios* (very large properties) the land in Galicia is divided (and subdivided) into tiny, often uneconomic individual holdings (*minifundios*), the result of

23

centuries of sharing out land between its owner's descendants. As a result you will frequently see people working in the fields (many of whom are women) doing tasks by hand that would elsewhere be done more economically by machine. Unlike parts of Navarre and Castille-León, too, where villages are often very far apart but whose buildings are tightly concentrated together, those in Galicia are often tiny, not far apart, and individually much more spread out so that you are not usually very far from a building of some kind. The region is also criss-crossed with a veritable maze of old green lanes, which wend their way through fields separated by stone boundaries made of large slabs set on end like rows of giant teeth, so that without some kind of waymarking system the *camino* would be almost impossible to follow. Another characteristic feature of the Galician countryside is the *hórreo*: a long rectangular granary of stone, or sometimes brick, raised up on pillars and used for storing potatoes and corncobs. They have slightly pitched roofs with a cross at one end, a decorative knob at the other. *Hórreos* vary greatly in length, from those that are only 3 or 4m long to enormous structures with two or three compartments and that stretch for 20 or 30m (the longest on record, some 150m from one end to the other, is in the village of San Martiño de Ozón, to the northwest of Finisterre).

Due to its location Galicia remained isolated from the influence

Hórreo (Photo: Ysabel Halpin)

Palloza (O Cebreiro) (Photo: Ysabel Halpin)

of much of what was happening to the rest of Spain in former centuries, and still retains evidence of its Celtic origins. The *palloza*, a round stone dwelling with a thatched roof, dates from these times and several are to be found in the village of O Cebreiro, while traditional Galician music uses the *gaita* (bagpipe). (Pilgrims interested in the architecture, working life and customs of Galicia should visit the Museo do Pobo Galego when they reach Santiago.)

Galicia is also a very heavily wooded area – many of the trees are centuries old – and as a result is very pleasant to walk in, even in the height of summer. Unfortunately, however, in recent years large areas of forest have been devastated by an epidemic of huge fires, suspected to have been started deliberately, but why or by whom no one really seems to know. Those who continue on to Finisterre will also see something of the Galician coastline, with its *rías*, the fjord-like inlets along the Atlantic coast from the border of Portugal to the province of Asturias on the Costa Verde.

BEFORE YOU GO

• Read up as much as you can about the Way – its history, art, architecture and geography – as well as other people's accounts of their journeys. Suggestions for further reading are given in Appendix C.
• If you are one of the many people walking the Way who are not already

25

Finisterre: almost the end of the world! (Photo: Paddy Dillon)

used to walking or used to carrying a rucksack day in, day out, get in plenty of practice before you go. Consider joining your local rambling club at least six months in advance and go out with them as often as you can. Most clubs have walks of different lengths and speeds so you can start with a shorter, slower one if you need to and gradually build up your speed and stamina. In this way you can benefit from walking with other people (usually friendly), walk in the countryside, have someone to lead who knows the way and suitable places to go (which you may not), and you can also practise walking in hilly places (which you will need). Then start increasing the amount of weight and luggage you take out with you until you can carry what you need. After that go out walking on at least two consecutive days on several occasions, in hilly places, carrying all your proposed gear with you: walking 30km on a 'one-off' basis is a very different matter from getting up again the following morning, probably stiff and possibly footsore, and starting out all over again. In this way you should have an enjoyable journey, with trouble-free feet and back.

• Don't expect *anybody* – anybody at all – to speak English! Assume you will have to speak Spanish all the time, according to where you are, for everything you need, however complicated. So if you are not already fairly fluent, consider a year's evening classes or home study with tapes in your preparations: you will find yourself extremely isolated if you cannot carry out practical transactions but also are unable to converse with the (very many) Spanish-speaking pilgrims and other people you will meet along the Way.

• Decide what type of footwear you will be taking – walking shoes, lightweight boots, heavy (thick-soled) trainers, and so on – and break them in *before* you go.

PLANNING YOUR SCHEDULE

As already indicated, the route from the Pyrenees to Santiago can be walked comfortably in four to five weeks by anyone who is fairly fit, leaving plenty of time to visit places of interest along the Way. Allow plenty of time when planning your itinerary, though, especially if you are not an experienced walker. Start with fairly short stages and always stop *before* you are tired. You can increase the distances as you get fitter and into the swing of things.

Try not to plan too tight a schedule, but allow plenty of time and flexibility to account for unforeseen circumstances (pleasant or otherwise). Where and how many rest days you take is up to you (though Burgos and León are 'musts'), as is also whether you include several short days walking in your programme, arriving at your destination during the late morning so as to have the remainder of the day completely free. If you are extremely tired, though, or having

27

trouble with your feet, a complete day off works wonders (particularly in a small place with no 'sights' to be visited) and is well worth the disruption to your schedule that it might initially seem. Allow at least three days to visit Santiago at the end – there is plenty to see and you will also meet up with many of the other walkers you have met along the Way.

EQUIPMENT

Rucksack: At least 50 litres if carrying a sleeping bag
Footwear: Both to walk in and a spare pair of lightweight trainers/sandals
Waterproofs: Even in summer it may rain, especially in Galicia. A *poncho* (a cape with a hood and space inside for a rucksack) is far more useful (and far less hot) than a cagoule or anorak
Pullover: Much of the route is high up and it can get cold at night, even in summer
First aid kit: (including a needle for draining blisters). Elastoplast sold by the metre is more useful than individual dressings. Scissors. High-factor sunscreen if you burn easily
Torch
Large water bottle: At least 2 litres if walking in July and August
Sleeping bag: Essential if staying in *refugios* in Spain as blankets are not usually provided
Sleeping mat: Useful if staying in *refugios*, where you may have to sleep on the floor, and also for siestas in the open air

Stick: Useful for fending off/frightening dogs and testing boggy terrain
Guidebook
Maps
Compass
Sun hat: (preferably with wide brim)
Small dictionary
Mug, spoon and knife

If you are addicted to tea/coffee, or can't get going in the morning without a hot drink, a 'camping gaz' type **stove** is a great advantage, even though it will add extra weight to your luggage. This is especially useful in summer when you will probably set out very early – 5.30 or 6am – to avoid the heat, since cafés and bars rarely open before 8.30 or 9am. Not all *refugios* have cooking facilities. (If you do take a camping gaz stove make sure it uses the 200g cylinders – smaller ones are not available in Spain.) To economise on weight/ space take a tin mug both to heat water in and drink out of. Alternatively, if all you want to do is heat water for a drink an electric plunger/mini-boiler type heater (with continental adaptor) is useful.

A **tent** is not normally worth the trouble as rooms are usually available (in bars and cafés) if you are not staying in *refugios*, and campsites in Spain can also be relatively expensive. However, if you are planning to walk in July or August a tent can often be useful (in villages) to camp in the grounds beside *refugios* where not only all the beds/bunks are full

Walking along an open hill track between Ponferrada and Villafranca del Bierzo (Photo: Paddy Dillon)

but where all other available space is occupied by people sleeping on the floor.

In general, travel as light as you can, not just for the weight but also, according to the season, because of the heat.

THERE AND BACK

How to Get There

Saint-Jean-Pied-de-Port: By train from Paris to Bayonne by TGV (or by coach direct from London) and then by local train (three to four times daily). Ryanair operates flights from London to Biarritz, with easy access to Bayonne railway station.

Roncesvalles: By bus from Pamplona bus station to Burguete (6pm, not Sundays) and then walk the remaining 3km along the road. In summer the service continues to Roncesvalles and also carries a limited number of bicycles (remove panniers first). (Check carefully in winter/early spring/late autumn as they sometimes only go as far as Zubiri.) In Spain each bus company has its own ticket office (*taquilla*): this route (terminating in Jaurrieta) is operated by 'La Montañesa'.

Pamplona: By train or coach from Madrid or Bilbao; by coach from London (Zaragoza service).

Madrid: By air direct from London; by train from London via Paris; by coach direct from London.

Bilbao: By air direct from London, then coach (to Pamplona, Logroño, Burgos).

Other places along the Way (for those who are only doing a section): Logroño, Burgos, León, Astorga and Ponferrada can all be reached by train from Madrid, though the coach (to all these places) may often be both quicker and more convenient (Spain has a very extensive, efficient long-distance coach network). Villafranca del Bierzo can also be reached directly by coach from both Madrid and Santiago, as can Pedrafita (for O Cebreiro). Burgos is on both the London–Madrid coach and the Paris–Madrid train routes.

How to Get Back from Santiago

Air: There are scheduled Iberia flights from Santiago to Heathrow (expensive). Otherwise go to Madrid by coach or train and fly from there.

Train: To Paris. Leaves at 9am everyday, arriving Hendaye late evening, in time for the connection overnight for Paris, arriving early the following morning.

Coach: To Paris, direct, two to three times a week, depending on the time of year. Cheaper, comfortable and slightly shorter than the train journey. The journey takes 24 hours and arrives at the Porte de Bagnolet bus station from where you can continue to London.

Accommodation

Various types of accommodation are available along the Way, ranging from luxurious five-star hotels (such as the state-run *paradores* established in redundant historic buildings) down to very basic *refugios* set up in schools and church halls.

Hotel (H) usually implies a higher standard of accommodation than that found in a *hostal* (Hs) which, in turn, normally offers more facilities than a *fonda* (F) (*hospedaje* in Galicia), a *casa de huéspedes* (CH) and, going down the scale, a *posada* (P). (*Residencia* after either a *hotel* or a *hostal* means it only provides accommodation: neither meals nor breakfast are available.) A number of bars also provide rooms (*habitaciones* – *camas* means 'beds'), so it is worth asking about these even if there isn't a sign or notice to say so. However, a word of warning if you intend to stay in any of these and want to leave early in the morning to avoid walking in the heat: make sure you arrange to pay the previous evening and retain your passport. You must also check how you will actually get out of the building the following morning (find out which doors or entrances will be locked and how they can be opened) or else you may find yourself unable to leave until at least 9am.

A *refugio* is simple accommodation set up especially for pilgrims on foot or by bicycle (but *not* for those accompanied by a back-up vehicle)

The hilltop village of Cirauqui in Navarra (Photo: Paddy Dillon)

THE WAY OF ST JAMES – THE PYRENEES – SANTIAGO – FINISTERRE

and is *only* for those holding a *credencial* or 'pilgrim passport' (see below). (This is to ensure that these facilities are not used by 'pseudo-pilgrims', hitch-hikers or backpacking travellers.) *Refugios* are provided by churches, religious orders, *ayuntamientos* (town halls or local authorities) and private individuals and are being set up in more and more places along the Way (and in Galicia in particular), especially since 1989, when the Pope visited Santiago. Literally thousands of people made the pilgrimage that year, either individually or in (sometimes huge) groups. Accommodation also increased in preparation for the very large numbers expected for the 1993 Holy Year when 99,000 pilgrims received their *compostelas*. Some *refugios* are in large towns, others in small villages; many are unmanned while others, increasingly, have volunteer wardens during the summer months. The facilities offered vary enormously, from those with beds/bunks, a kitchen and hot showers, down to those with only a cold tap and in which you will have to sleep on the floor without a mattress. Note, however, that *refugios* are *not* provided as cheap substitutes for hotels but as alternatives to sleeping rough, places to shelter pilgrims from the elements, and so you cannot expect anything other than that they are clean and that the facilities offered function properly. Some are very large, others very small, some operate in the summer only, and in

July and August they may be *extremely* crowded since no one ever seems to be turned away. Many charge a fixed fee, whilst others are still technically free of charge, but you should always offer to pay and there is usually a box for donations towards their upkeep, especially those run by religious or charitable bodies. Note, however, that you cannot reserve a place in a *refugio* in advance and that they operate on a strictly 'first come first served' basis.

However, since the availability of these facilities varies greatly from year to year details may change, and for up-to-date information it is advisable to obtain the annually revised guide published by the Confraternity of St James. Unlike *hotels, fondas* and so on, you will not normally encounter any difficulty in leaving *refugios* early and will find that most other people are doing the same.

Planning the Day

Long-distance walkers in Britain usually operate on a 'nine-to-five' basis, leaving their accommodation shortly after breakfast and returning in time for an early evening meal. There may be few, if any, places of historical, religious or cultural interest directly on the path (such as churches, cathedrals or stately homes) that require a detailed indoor visit (as opposed to historic bridges, fortifications, market crosses and so on that can be inspected fairly quickly from the outside), and those that do normally work

Boots, boots and yet more boots (Photo: Ysabel Halpin)

'nine-to-five' as well so that combining walking and sightseeing is usually incompatible. Walkers in Britain, in the main, tend just to walk. In Spain, however, not only are there an enormous number of places of outstanding artistic, architectural, cultural or religious interest well worth visiting along the Way of St James, but they are also open at convenient times for the walker: as well as 10am to 1pm, they normally open again in the evenings from 4 or 5pm to 7 or 8pm. Churches, except in big towns, are usually closed all day, unless there is a service going on. However, it is often possible to visit during Saturday afternoons when they are being cleaned in preparation for Sunday.

In July and August in particular it is *extremely* hot during the day, with temperatures often in the high 90s, and there is very little shade on the *camino*, apart from many areas of Galicia. When walking in hot weather it is important to avoid becoming dehydrated by drinking plenty of water *before* you set out; once you realise you haven't had enough to drink it is too late to do anything about it, even if you have supplies with you (top up your water bottle whenever you can). It is difficult to do but if you can drink *at least* half a litre of water as soon as you get up (as well as any tea/coffee available) you will find the hot weather affects you much less. The best way to avoid walking in the heat is to get up before it is light and set out at daybreak. At this time of day it is cool and pleasant, with the added advantages of watching the sun rise as you walk and enjoying the scenery in the early morning light. In this way, even with stops, you should be able to reach your destination by

33

the early afternoon, when you can then rest up awhile before going out sightseeing/visiting in the (relative) cool of the early evening. It is also a good idea, in large towns and other places of any size, to go for a walk in the evening and check how you will leave, so as not to waste time or get lost the following morning.

If you do decide to continue walking in the evening, after lunch and a siesta, make sure that you have no more than 10km left to go.

Other Practical Information

Shops: Shops (for food) are usually open between 9 or 10am and 2pm and then again between 5 and 8pm or later. In small villages they are not always marked, and you may have to ask where these are (though in such places bars often double up as shops) and be prepared for them not to be well stocked: in remote places the lines carried are often only very basic and limited in range. Except for large supermarkets in big towns, food shops close on Saturday afternoon and all day Sunday, though bakers are often open on Sunday mornings if you can find them. Unlike France (where they are very numerous and easily seen), in Spain there is usually only one in each village or district, they may not always be marked, and may only have a small entrance on the street leading to the large baking area behind.

Public holidays: There are more of these in Spain (*días festivos*) than in

Britain: 1 January, Good Friday, 15 August, 1 November, 5, 6 and 25 December. There are also three others which are taken locally and therefore vary from one area to another, as well as (especially in August) the *fiestas* in honour of a town or village's own patron saint and which can last up to a week in some places (Estella, for example). Shops, including those for food (but not bars or restaurants) will be closed on these occasions.

Meals in Spain are much later than in Britain: 2 to 3.30pm for lunch and 8.30 or 9pm until 11pm for evening dinner. However, as most bars also provide *tapas* (different kinds of snacks, both hot and cold) as well as (in many) *bocadillos* (sandwiches) you need not go hungry if you are feeling ravenous outside regular mealtimes. Breakfast, in hotels, *fondas*, and so on, is rarely available before 9am.

Cafés and bars close very late but do not normally open before 8.30 or 9am, and in small villages do not always serve hot drinks all day long. Remember that a 'cafetería' in Spain is not a self-service restaurant but a bar that also serves things to eat for breakfast (such as cake, sandwiches or hot *tapas*).

Changing money: Banks are only open from 8.30am till 2pm and on Saturday mornings in large towns only, but you can change money in all post offices displaying the 'Deutsche bank' sign. However, there are also cash dispensers (*cajeros automáticos*) in all places of any size and which accept a very wide selection of cards.

Post offices: These are known as *correos* and are often open in the mornings only, but stamps (as well as single envelopes) can also be bought in *estancos* (tobacconists).

Poste restante: If you want to send things to yourself further along the route (such as maps and guides), or have people write to you, use the *poste restante* system whereby you collect your mail (on presentation of your passport) at the post office. In Spain this service is called *Lista de Correos*, is free, and items are kept for you for a month before they are returned to the sender.

Address the letter/parcel to yourself, Lista de Correos, street address, postal code and name of town: for example, Joe Bloggs, Lista de Correos, Paseo Sarasate 9, 31080 Pamplona.

The places you will be most likely to need are the following: Paseo Sarasate 9, 31080 PAMPLONA; Plaza San Agustín 1, 26080 LOGROÑO; Plaza Conde de Castro 1, 09080 BURGOS; Jardines de San Francisco s/n, 24080 LEON; Alférez Provisional 3, 24700 ASTORGA; Calle General Vives 1, 24400 PONFERRADA; Calle Calvo Sotelo 183, 27600 SARRIA; Travesia Fonseca s/n, 15780 SANTIAGO DE COMPOSTELA. Also, if you

decide (while in Spain) that you have too much in your rucksack it is considerably cheaper to post it to yourself this way in Santiago than to send a parcel home to Britain. Make sure, however, when collecting such items, that the clerk looks not only under your surname (*apellido*) but also under your first name (*nombre*); as the Spanish system of surnames is different you may find your mail has been filed in the wrong place.

Telephones: In Spain (which has one of the most expensive telephone systems in Europe) phone boxes usually take both coins and phone cards (*tarjeta telefonica*), obtainable from post offices and many *estancos*. Most Spanish area codes begin with a '9', which is now included when calling from abroad. The emergency number for the Guardia Civil is 062, 112 for other emegencies.

Telephone books (*guía telefónica*) are by province (white and yellow pages in separate books) and entries are arranged by town or population centre so that it is easy to locate hotels and *fondas* in a specific place. Postcodes are also included.

As **mobile phones** frequently do not work in rural areas and as there are plenty of easily accessible telephone boxes (*cabina telefónica*) all along the *camino* it is suggested that you leave your mobile at home. You will also find it a much more 'pilgrim' journey if your friends and relations cannot contact you (rather than you ringing them) to tell you, for example, that the central heating doesn't work, that the cat next door has been run over or that your mother-in-law has broken her spectacles...

Medical assistance: Make sure that you obtain a **Form E111** from the post office before leaving Britain. This is a Europe-wide document entitling you to free medical (but not dental) treatment under the Spanish health system.

If you wear glasses all the time it is suggested that you take either a spare pair or the prescription with you.

Stamps for pilgrim passports: Modern pilgrims who seek proof of their pilgrimage also carry pilgrim 'passports' (*credencial* in Spanish) which they have stamped at regular intervals along the Way (churches, town halls and so on) and which they then present to the Cathedral authorities in Santiago to help them obtain their *compostela* or certificate. They are also *essential* if you wish to sleep in *refugios*. More information about this is available from the Confraternity of St James. They can also be obtained (in person) from the monastery authorities in Roncesvalles and in some (but not all) larger *refugios* along the way.

Masses are usually at 12 noon or 1pm on Sundays, 8pm on Saturday evening for Sunday and in places of any size there is frequently a service on Monday to Friday evenings at 8pm as well.

Dogs, their owners nearly always tell you, 'won't hurt you', though this is often hard to believe. They may tell you, too, that it is the rucksack that bothers them (and as dogs are reputed to see only in black and white there may be some truth in this, faced with mysterious hump-backed monsters on two legs...) but it is not much comfort when faced with an aggressive one. Reports vary as to how troublesome they are, and some recent pilgrims have suggested that with the increasing popularity of the *camino* they are no longer as annoying as they used to be. But they do live all along the route, frequently running around loose, hear you ages before you have any idea where they are and are often enormous (though the small ones are, in fact, a greater nuisance, as they have a nasty habit of letting you pass quietly by and then attacking from behind, nipping you in the back of your ankles). A **stick** is very useful, even though you might not normally want to walk with one – not to hit them with but to threaten. Be warned!

Hunting season: When this opens (1 October onwards) be particularly vigilant when walking through areas with either trees or scrubby terrain and stick firmly to the paths, especially at weekends and on public holidays when shooting birds, rabbits and so on is a very popular activity.

Chapel at the monastery at Roncesvalles (Photo: Paddy Dillon)

USING THIS GUIDE

Waymarking

The route described in this book begins in Saint-Jean-Pied-de-Port and follows the waymarked *Camino francés* in Spain, ending first at the Cathedral in Santiago de Compostela (in the direction of the [modern] pilgrimage), and then, for those who wish to continue to 'the end of the earth', at Finisterre on the coast. It is therefore described in one direction only. Pilgrims who would like to walk the Way in reverse, or return on foot, will find it difficult since its waymarking is also 'one way only'. For this reason some hints have been included in the text [in square brackets] as the *camino* is often difficult to follow backwards, even if you have already walked the outward journey. This is why, from time to time, the

text contains such seemingly irrelevant remarks as 'track joins from back L' (redundant for those walking only towards Santiago but helpful for the person going in reverse and faced with a choice of paths).

Waymarking (*señalización*) is, as indicated above, in one direction only (towards Santiago and then on to Finisterre) and is in the form of yellow arrows (*flechas*) or flashes (*señales*) which are painted on tree trunks, walls, road signs, rocks, the ground, sides of buildings and so on, and are normally extremely easy to spot. They appear at frequent intervals and the walker will not usually encounter any difficulty following them, except in some areas where road construction is in progress. (If, at any time, they seem to have disappeared, this will be because you have inadvertently taken

Yellow arrow and Council of Europe waymark tiles (Photo: Ysabel Halpin)

Pinman waymark

a wrong turning: retrace your steps to the last one you saw and start again from there, checking carefully.) Some sections are also waymarked with blue-and-white metal signs bearing the picture of a pilgrim in a hat, while the beginning part, as far as Viana, has the red-and-white *balises* of the French GR system as well, as a continuation of the route from Le Puy. In Galicia, in addition, there are standardised concrete marker stones, about the size of old-fashioned milestones, bearing an embossed conch-shell design, the number of kilometres remaining to Santiago (not always accurate) and the name of the village, hamlet or spot where they are located. They are positioned at 500m intervals and are not only attractive, providing reassurance that you are on the right

track (as indicated above, Galicia is criss-crossed with literally hundreds of old 'green lanes', involving constant changes of direction in some places) but are also a useful way of knowing exactly where you are in villages that are too small to bear the usual place-name signs. It is apparently planned, eventually, to extend this type of *señal* to the rest of the *camino*.

Maps

These are a problem in Spain. It is possible to follow the *camino* just with the waymarks and this guide, but that would be very limiting. Maps are useful not merely as a means of finding the way when lost but also for locating the walk in the context of its surroundings and for making any diversions to visit places of interest within striking distance of the route. At present there are no comprehensive, reliable Spanish equivalents of the Ordnance Survey maps of Britain or the French IGN series. In 1989, however, the Spanish IGN *(Instituto Nacional Geográfico)*, in conjunction with MOPT *(Ministerio de Obras Públicas y Transportes)*, published a map entitled *El Camino de Santiago*, covering the whole of the *Camino francés* on a scale of 1:600.000. This is not detailed enough to walk from but situates the *camino* in the context of its surroundings and is readily available (from Stanfords map shop in London, for example, or The Map Shop, Upton-upon-Severn – see Appendix D). Otherwise two maps in the Michelin 1,400.000 (1cm: 4km) orange series are recommended: 441 North West Spain and 442 Northern Spain. It is for this reason that sketch maps of the route are included with this text.

Textual Description

The route is divided into several sections (eg. Burgos to León), the end point of each being a place where the walker can reach or leave the route easily by public transport if they wish to complete the route in shorter stages. Each of the main places along the route appears in green; they are preceded by the distance walked from the previous one and followed by a description of the facilities available, a brief history, where applicable, and an indication of the places of interest to visit. (Walkers wishing to spend time in any of the larger towns should obtain information leaflets and a street plan from the Tourist Office there.) The text is not divided up into stages as in this way the walker can decide for him or herself the distances he or she would like to cover each day, but places offering accommodation are preceded by a house symbol. (It is suggested that you go through the text in advance and mark possible overnight stops with a highlight pen.) The figures after each place-name heading indicate the height in metres where known and, in parentheses, the distance in kilometres from both Saint-Jean-Pied-de-Port and Santiago. In the case of large towns (Pamplona, Burgos, for example) the

distances to/from them start/end in their centres, usually at the cathedral.

Place names appear in the text in **bold type**, as do other names that help in wayfinding, such as street names, the names of prominent buildings, rivers, and so on. However, 'river', in Spain, rarely implies a wide, deep, fast-flowing stretch of navigable water: most, if not actually dried up, are no more than narrow trickles at the bottom of a wide river bed and may be non-existent at certain times of the year.

Abbreviations have been kept to a minimum. L indicates that you should turn/fork left, R that you should turn/fork R. (L) and (R) mean that something you pass is to your left or right. KSO = Keep Straight On. // = parallel. Km = kilometre, KM = kilometre marker (found on the sides of all main roads; K is reserved for the marker stones in Galicia). N followed by a number (N135) refers to the number of a main road, C (or the first two initials of the province you are in, for example, LU = Lugo) to one of a local road. RENFE is the abbreviation for the Spanish national railway network.

Unlike pilgrimages to Lourdes, Fatima or other locations where miracles are sought and help for specific problems requested, and where being in the pilgrim destination itself is the most important factor, on the Way of St James it is the making of the journey itself that is the pilgrim's principal concern, the arrival in Santiago being only a conclusion to the rest of the undertaking. It is not a 'map and compass route', either, though there are a couple of stiff climbs (for example over the Pyrenees, and up to O Cebreiro as you enter Galicia). Timings have not been given from place to place but 4km per hour, exclusive of stops, is often considered average, especially when carrying a heavy rucksack. However, a comfortable pace may often be more than this: a fit walker may well be able to maintain a speed of 5 to 6km or 3.5 miles per hour.

The route is practicable, though not necessarily recommended, all through the year. In winter there is nearly always a lot of snow in the Pyrenees and it rains a lot in the Basque country. The weather may be dry over much of the route through Castille and León, but as a lot of it is quite high up (Burgos, for instance, is at 610m, though the area around it is more or less flat) it gets very cold, with a biting wind. In spring it rains a lot, especially in Galicia (Santiago has the highest average rainfall in Spain) and in Navarre. If you are not restricted to a particular time of year, May/early June or the autumn are best: dry, but not as hot as in summer, with long hours of daylight, and accommodation is much less crowded. Traditionally, though, as many people as possible aimed to arrive in Santiago for the festivities on 25 July, St James's Day, particularly in Holy Years. Many people still do.

¡Ultreya!

Porte Saint-Jacques, Saint-Jean-Pied-de-Port (Photo: Ysabel Halpin)

THE ROUTE
Saint-Jean-de-Pied-de-Port to Roncesvalles

☎ 4km Saint-Jean-Pied-de-Port (Donibarne Garazi) 180m (0/778)

Population 1400. All facilities, seven hotels, several *chambres d'hôte* (B&B), campsite by river (1/4–15/10). Two *gîtes d'étape*: a) Mme Etchegoin, 9 Rue d'Huart (05.59.37.12.08, 12pl), b) (pilgrims only) Rue de la Citadelle (16pl, March–Nov, access via Accueil Pèlerin). Pilgrim information office (Acceuil Pèlerin de l'Association des Amis de Saint-Jacques des Pyrénées Atlantiques) is run by volunteers, mainly former pilgrims, at 39 Rue de la Citadelle, open March–Nov, early morning to evening, and provides information on the route in Spain and helps with accommodation; it is suggested you call there as soon as you arrive in St Jean-Pied-de-Port. Tourist Office, SNCF (to Bayonne).

This is 'Saint-John-at-the-Foot-of-the-Pass', a small border town on the river Nive, capital of the Basque province of Basse Navarre with an ancient cobbled *haute ville*. Several places of interest: Citadelle, overlooking the town, with its system of ramparts: access either from the top end of the Rue de la Citadelle or by staircase (*escalier de la poterne*) leading up from the footpath along the river by the side of the church – worth the climb on a clear day. Prison des Evêques, Musée de la Pelote, 14th-century Eglise Notre-Dame-du-bout-du-pont ('Our Lady at the end of the bridge') part of the former priory-hospital. Pont Romain, the different 'portes' (Saint Jacques, d'Espagne, for example). Note architecture of Basque-style houses with often ornate wooden overhangs at roof level, balconies. If you have time to spare the Tourist Office has a booklet of waymarked walks in the area.

Traditionally pilgrims entered the town by the Porte Saint Jacques at the top of the Rue de la Citadelle and those who have followed the GR65 from Le Puy on places along this route will have done the same. After that there were two routes to Roncesvalles. The older one, following the course of the river Valcarlos, is now the modern road (D933 in France, N135 in Spain). This route is no shorter but is not so steep. It is on the main road for most of the first 15km but if the weather is very bad or visibility poor you should take this. (*Gîte d'é-tape* 4km out of Saint-Jean-Pied-de-Port on this route, at Moulin de Fargas, 05.59.37.12.54m, 22pl).

The other, high-level *Route Napoléon* was the one he took to cross into Spain, following existing tracks already used by shepherds and pilgrims for

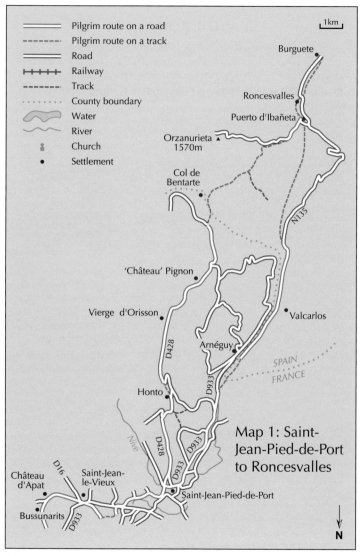

Map 1: Saint-Jean-Pied-de-Port to Roncesvalles

several centuries. This leads over the Pyrenees via the Col de Bentarte and the Port de Cize, continuing along the path of the old Roman road from Bordeaux to Astorga, and is normally accessible without any trouble (such as too much snow) from May to October. It is 26km long and is a spectacular route on a clear day but do not attempt it if it is already very windy down below in Saint-Jean-Pied-de-Port; higher up you can experience force nine gales and appalling weather, even in the height of summer. (Note, however, that there is a *gîte d'étape* plus B&B 5km out of Saint-Jean, at Honto.)

The *Route Napoléon* was also the one favoured by pilgrims in centuries gone by because, although it was much more strenuous, it was also exposed for most of the way, and ambush by bandits was thus less likely than on the densely wooded route through Valcarlos. If you are a fairly fit walker allow at least seven hours actual walking (excluding stops); if not, allow much longer, especially if it is windy (when it will almost always be against you).

However, whichever route you take start early in the day (6.30am in summer or as soon as it is light), not only to avoid the heat but also to avoid being high up later in the day when the light is fading and you are tired. If you choose the Route Napoléon take *enough food and water* with you and (both routes) the following morning's breakfast.

A: ROUTE NAPOLEON

The Route Napoléon *is the continuation of the GR65 over the Pyrenees. It is now tarmacked as the D428 until just before the Col de Bentarte, but is normally very quiet, with little traffic except at weekends when the hunting season opens in October. Start early in the day as the first 16km are continuously uphill, although, as explained above, it is possible to shorten this stretch by 5km by leaving Saint-Jean-Pied-de-Port later in the day and spending the night in either the* gîte d'étape *or B&B at Honto (see below).*

Go down the **Rue de la Citadelle**, past the church of **Notre-Dame-du-bout-du-pont** *(fountain)*, through the **Porte d'Espagne**, cross the bridge over the river **Nive** and KSO on up the **Rue d'Espagne**. Continue ahead up the **Route Saint-Michel**.

This is clearly waymarked with both yellow flashes and/or arrows (these flechas amarillas *will continue all through Spain too) as well as with scallop shells, and is easy to follow; you keep on the D428 all the time, ignoring turns, apart from a few occasions (indicated in the text) when you short-cut some of its many 'hairpins'.*

Continue up the **Route Saint-Michel** for about 100m, bear L at a fork, and after 20m you will come to a junction with the **Route Maréchal Harrispe**. Take this (bear R off the **Route Saint-Michel**, which bends round to the L). *(Fountain on L.)*

45

Route Napoléon, 'only 765 km left to go to Santiago...' (Photo: Ysabel Halpin)

KSO and after about 500m there is a small junction and the road name changes to **Route Napoléon.**

Follow the road as it winds (mostly) up and (sometimes) down, past small roadside farms. At fork bear L. KSO following road all the time *(but keep turning round from time to time to admire the view – after this there is nothing as steep until you climb up to O Cebreiro and enter Galicia). At this level there are still trees to provide some shade.* Pass a T-junction (**Maison Etchébestia**, 302m), and KSO. About 100m further on, road forks at massive tree (good place for a rest) – keep R *(fork to L goes down to village of Saint-Michel)* and KSO to...

☎ 5km Honto (Huntto) 540m (5/773)

Gîte d'étape (Ferme Ithurburia, 05.59.37.11.17, 25pl), also B&B.

About 50m after passing **Honto** the road veers R but the GR65 bears L up a grassy track (the old road), leaving the modern road for a while (to rejoin it later) making a short cut via the old, steep route that zigzags between walls/banks at first and then on open ground.

The waymarks are mainly painted on rocks on the ground in this section, but if you have difficulty in seeing them (for example in snow) you can spot the place where you will meet the road again (a) by a tap on the RH side of the road and (b) by two small houses L and R of the road – the one on your R is called Arbol Azopian.

The path joins the road again (at 710m) after eight or nine 'hairpins'.

[NB If you are walking towards Saint-Jean-Pied-de-Port – going back – leave the road to your R after the tap on your L, dropping down by a drystone wall and walking alongside it. This turn is well marked on a large rock at RH side of the road before you leave it.]

From here you can see over the mountains to the east towards the frequently snow-covered peaks of the Col de Somport, Mont d'Aspe and so on.

KSO on road, ignoring tracks to either L or R. When you see a farm building off to the L where a stream crosses under the road, the road veers round to the R and shortly afterwards, after three or four more hairpins, flattens out and you reach the...

6km Vierge d'Orisson 1095m (11/767)

A small statue of the Virgin Mary – brought here from Lourdes by shepherds – in a prominent position at the side of a road junction and in a level area. Panoramic views and a good place for a rest (not too long).

At the Vierge d'Orisson you are halfway in time (but not in distance) between Saint-Jean-Pied-de-Port and Roncesvalles. It is still 5km to the border and the route still climbs, though less steeply now, up to the Col de Bentarte, after which it is nearly all downhill. The temperature may be cooler as you climb higher but the sun, if it is out, will still be as hot.

Be careful to take the R fork here (the LH option leads you back down again!) and continue on road (having taken R fork) and KSO at road junction (with the D128, R, to Arnéguy). At 1177m pass the 'remains' of **Château Pignon** (L). Ignore a turn to L after 300m and also a fork to R after 300m (to a farm 100m off road).

Continue on road until it begins to veer round to L, at which point the *camino* leaves the road (at 1240m) up a clearly marked grassy track by the **Croix Thibaut**, *a modern wayside cross erected in 1990 on the RH side of the road with an inscription in Basque ('I am the way...').* This path takes you towards the pass above on the rocky summit of **Leizar-Atheka** (1300m). Since the road veers L you are in effect continuing more or less in a straight line, although you actually walk off the road to the R.

The road continues for another 3km to the border at the Col d'Arnostéguy, more or less on the level, before it turns left back downhill again. However, if you get caught unexpectedly in foggy weather you can continue along this road and then backtrack along the border fence until you reach marker no 199 and where the terrain is slightly shaded: see below.

Climb up between the two very large rocks, after which the path begins to descend. Pass border marker stone no 198 (1290m) and then follow the border fence (above the forest below to the R) to marker no 199 (1344m). About 120m after this you cross a cattle grid through the fence into...

5km Spain (16/762)

You may find remains of snow here, even in early June.

The grassy track veers round to the R, past a tumbledown house (L) at the **Col de Bentarte** (1330m). Continue along path through beechwoods. Pass sheep pen and hut on R. Do not take R fork here but KSO back into the woods again (well waymarked).

When you come out of the woods again the track falls away to the R *(good views)* but KSO (don't fork R here). About 10m further on track forks left but KSO (take R fork).

Over to your L you will now be able to see the TV mast on Monte Orzanzurieta (1570m).

'Border crossing' on the Route Napoléon (France and Spain) (Photo: Ysabel Halpin)

From here the path winds (mostly) up for 1–2km to meet the road at the...

4.5km Col Lepoeder 1440m (20.5/757.5)

From here you have the first, plunging, view of the rooftops of the abbey at Roncesvalles down in the valley below, the village of Burguete and, on a clear day, right across into the province of Navarra.

There are in fact two routes down to Roncesvalles, one via the Puerta de Ibañeta *and the other, very steep, via the* Calzada Romana *(old Roman road), which drops down to the monastery directly, straight ahead, passing to the L of the hill known as Don Simon. This has been re-waymarked and is now the 'standard' route. Both are described here.*

a) For the 'short, sharp' route KSO ahead (following the marker stones) at the **Col Lepoeder** to the road, cross it and descend, forking L, into the woods. This is well waymarked so watch out carefully for the yellow arrows and the red-and-white *balises* as there are no distinguishing features to orient yourself. It descends very steeply all the time, describing a 'J'-shaped loop, straight down to the abbey, dropping over 500m in only 3.5km. At the bottom turn R to enter the abbey from the west (the back, *fountain*). Cross diagonally through a courtyard and pass in front of the church in **Roncesvalles** (4km) (see page 51).

b) The alternative *(and recommended for people with bad knees)* is to follow the road, which you join by taking a short path R off the road you are on after the col and follow it down (there are a few short cuts through its hairpins) to the **Puerto d'Ibañeta 1057m** (4km). *Continue as described on page 51.*

B: VALCARLOS ROUTE

From the **Rue de la Citadelle** go through the **Porte d'Espagne** (passing the church on your L, *fountain*), cross the bridge over the river **Nive**, go up the **Rue d'Espagne** but then turn R into the **Rue d'Uhart**. Continue along **Place Floquet** (under the *jardin public*), through the rampart gateway and then, after 20m, bear L when you see a signpost to 'Arnéguy 8'. Follow the road until the group of *ventas (originally country inns but nowadays duty-free-type shops)* 2km before Arnéguy.

If you walk this section on a Sunday (when there are no heavy goods vehicles) there will be considerably less traffic than there is during the week.

Cross the bridge over the river **Nive** towards shops then turn L (old waymarks) onto what was formerly the old main road, passing to the RH side of the river, well above it. This is an old tarred lane, undulating along the side of the hill and very easy to follow. It brings you out on the Spanish side of the bridge in the border town of...

8km Arnéguy

Bars, more *ventas*.

KSO(R) on the N135 until...

🏘 3km Valcarlos (Luzaide) 365m

Border town on the Spanish side, with shops, Tourist Office, two banks (one with CD), hotel, *pensión*, bars and restaurants. Church of Santiago contains a life-size representation of Santiago Matamoros.

This section of the road is waymarked from time to time, both with yellow arrows and red-and-white balises. Unless it is foggy the 12km off-road section after road KM 56 is worth taking, as it is not only shorter than continuing on the N135 but also much quieter. There are not all that many waymarks but it is easy enough to follow.

KSO on N135, crossing **Río Chapitel**, and continue until shortly before road KM 57 where you fork L along gravel track (waymarked) downhill, crossing an old stone bridge over a small river at the bottom. Shortly after going through a gate watch out carefully as you then leave the track (which continues to a farm at the end) and fork R uphill on a FP. This undulates along the side of the hill, with splendid views on a clear day.

When track goes uphill again fork *hard* R (by a *camino* bollard) then *hard* L up grassy lane, leading uphill.

When the electric pylons turn R, KSO(L) on forest track, veering R through beechwoods, winding its way up to a junction of similar tracks (marked with another *camino* bollard). Turn L, veering R then L uphill to emerge on N135 at bend by small farm.

Turn L and 50m later turn L down shady level lane through woods, rising gently at first and then more steeply as grassy track winds its way along the side of the hill, following the line of the electric pylons. This section is very easy to follow and brings you out on a minor road to L of the N135, just before the chapel and orientation table at the...

13km Puerto d'Ibañeta 1057m

As related in the 10th-century narrative poem *Chanson de Roland*, the hero of this name, Count of Brittany and Charlemagne's nephew, attempted to resist the rear guard of the Saracen army at a famous battle in the Pyrenees in 778, single-handed and with only his faithful sword Durendal to defend himself. Too proud to blow his horn (the *olifant*) to summon assistance as instructed, he only did so after he had been mortally wounded. The Puerto d'Ibañeta is where Charlemagne and his retreating army had got to when they heard the sound of Roland's horn – too late to go back to help him. A bell used to toll at the original chapel to guide pilgrims in bad weather.

The modern *ermita* (chapel) of San Salvador was built in 1965 to replace the earlier ruined chapel of Charlemagne, with a sign in French, Spanish, Basque and Latin inviting pilgrims to pray to Notre-Dame de Roncevaux. It is usually locked, but you can see inside through the apertures in the door; the interior is very plain but has some nice stained-glass windows, best seen with the sunlight behind them. Outside altar for outdoor masses. There is also a modern monument nearby to Roland (Roldán in Spanish).

Cross road and go up mound ahead to chapel.

From here you walk through the woods for the last 2km to Roncesvalles. Go down FP to RH side of small white building to your L and follow it gently downhill all the time. Shortly before you get to the abbey you are joined by a track coming from the L, after which you enter the rear of the monastery *(fountain)*. Cross diagonally through a courtyard and pass in front of the church in **Roncesvalles** (7km).

♞ 4.5km Roncesvalles (Orreaga) 925m (25/753)

Shop with guidebooks and so on, hotel-restaurant, monastery-run *posada* (cash dispenser in lobby), youth hostel. Walker pilgrims may stay in the somewhat spartan refuge in the old hospital building (60+pl, open all year, manned by volunteer wardens Easter–Nov) after obtaining their *credencial* or pilgrim passport from the monastery authorities.

Augustinian monastery and hospital founded early in the 12th century. Set in the 'valley of thorns' in the foothills of the Pyrenees it has a long tradition of looking after pilgrims (it fed 25,000 a year during the 17th century). Collegiate church (evening mass followed by pilgrim blessing Easter–Nov),

Refugio in Roncesvalles (Photo: Ysabel Halpin)

chapel of Santiago, 14th-century royal pantheon containing the 13th-century tombs of Sancho the Strong and his wife Doña Clemencia of Toulouse. Museum with religious paintings and sculpture, treasury.

Roncesvalles to Burgos

The section from Roncesvalles to shortly before the outskirts of Pamplona is shady in the main and so can be walked comfortably even in July/August unless you are unusually affected by the heat.

Leave the monastery by the main entrance (KM 47 on the N135) and just after the Roncesvalles signboard fork R along shady, wide FP through trees, more or less // to road. After 1.5km turn L onto minor road by industrial buildings and then turn R onto N135 by Guardia Civil barracks at entrance *(picnic tables opposite)* to…

🏠 3km Burguete (Auritz) 893m (28/750)

Several *hostales*, two bars, two restaurants, bank, pharmacy.

Basque village with splendid 18th-/early 19th-century houses with armorial devices on either side of the main street.

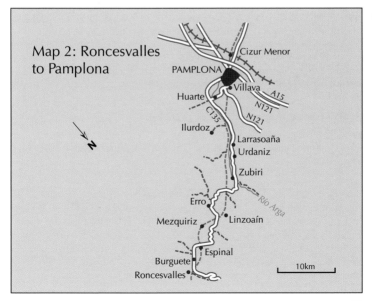

Map 2: Roncesvalles to Pamplona

Shady section of the camino in Navarra (Photo: Ysabel Halpin)

KSO down main street past modern church of **San Nicolás de Bari** and public garden and turn R 100m later along the side of the bank building. Cross FB over stream and 200m later turn L over bridge onto minor road. KSO (road becomes a track) then after 1km go through gate, cross two streams, and continue on wide gravel FP through woods, gradually uphill. At top, at crossing of similar tracks in clearing, KSO ahead downhill on earth road to N135 by (modern) church of **San Bartolomé** and tower of the **Biblioteca Pública** in…

4km Espinal (Aurizberri) 871m (32/746)

Shop, two bars, *panadería*, restaurant.

Basque village founded in 1269; houses with armorial devices above doorways.

Turn R on road through village. After passing fountain (on L) turn L at house no 19 (called **Aunta Mendi**) onto minor tarred road uphill. About 200m later KSO(L) at fork onto unsurfaced road; 100m later fork R onto FP leading into the woods, uphill all the time, via steps, to the top. *(View to rear over foothills to TV mast at Monte Orzanzurieta and Col Lepoeder.)* Fork R at top, turn L through gate and continue R along gravel lane and then KSO by fence along side of field. Go through gate at end and under trees and cross the road (carefully) at…

1.5km Alto de Mezquiriz (Puerto de Espinal) 922m (33.5/744.5)

A trilingual stele invites the pilgrim, in French, Spanish and Basque, to pray to Notre-Dame de Roncevaux.

After crossing the road do *not* go straight on through the gate and up the track, even though it might seem the most obvious path, but turn L, before you reach the fence, down a small FP, leading downhill, via a gate, into the woods. Go through gate at bottom, turn L and at bend in road go up sunken/hollow lane and 200m later emerge onto a wide, paved *piste* (like a cycle track). KSO(L) along it downhill for 1km to bend in main road. Turn R along concrete path, cross river and minor road and continue on another paved *piste* on RH side of N135 to old main road in village of…

3km Viscarret (Biskarreta) (36.5/741.5)

Small village with shop, bar; the end of the first stage of the Way of St James as outlined in the *Codex Calixtinus*. (It began in Saint Michel-le-Vieux, 3km south of Saint-Jean-Pied-de-Port.)

Turn R, veering L, cross N135, and continue through village, veering R. Fork L at end (just before returning to N135 and next to shop on L) down paved *piste*. At top of hill, by cemetery, take RH of two left forks (11 o'clock position) downhill through woods on gravel FP. Return to road after bend. Cross over and fork R on other side on similar track. KSO into main street in…

2km Linzoan (38.5/739.5)

Church on hill to L is a good place for a rest – shady, with good views.

From here to the Alto de Erro the route climbs uphill and then along a wooded ridge.
    Follow road through village past *frontón*, veer L *(fountain)*, then turn R uphill under footbridge over road and KSO upwards on stony walled lane. At crossing with gravel lane KSO ahead then 100m later fork R up stony FP into woods, levelling out, and then KSO(L) on wider track coming from back R. About 100m later fork R up narrow stony FP. Just before you reach a minor gravel road turn L onto rocky walled lane. Cross gravel road and KSO(L), veering L ahead, down another shady, stony lane.
    KSO on ridge, undulating, and ignoring turns, passing stone marked '*pasos de Roldán*'. It was in this section that Roland (*Roldán* in Spanish) eventually

55

decided – too late – to blow his horn to summon help from Charlemagne and his army, as related in the Song of Roland.

Continue ahead for 2km more, pass TV/radio masts and 100m later reach the road (C135) at...

5.5km Alto de Erro (Puerto de Erro) 801m (44/734)

Cross the road *(the stone construction opposite covers a former well, much used by pilgrims)* and continue ahead down wide gravelled lane, descending gradually at first.

After 1km pass to the L of an old building: this is the **Venta del Caminante** or **Venta del Puerto,** *a former pilgrim inn (posada del peregrino).* Continue downhill, more and more steeply, on very rocky, uneven path, watching out carefully for the waymarks all the time *(view of Zubiri ahead with its large magnesita factory).* Follow the track as it gradually loses height, descending to the old medieval bridge over the **Arga** in...

🏛 3.5km Zubiri 526m (47.5/730.5)

Bar, restaurant (rooms), shop, bank, *panadería, refugio.*

The name Zubiri means 'village with the bridge' in Basque. The bridge itself was known as *el puente de la rabia* because, so the story goes, any animal that crossed it three times was cured of rabies. The large building immediately to the R before you cross the bridge was a former hospital, possibly a leprosarium.

From Zubiri to just before Arre the camino follows the valley of the river Arga, crossing it (and back again) a couple of times.

If you want to go into the village cross the bridge *(fountain on other side, next to church).* Otherwise, turn L along path just before it (waymarked). Go up hill and down side of large house down lane, cross stream by footbridge and KSO on other side, veering round to R. At T-junction with gravel road near factory turn R along it downhill, then L on a tarmac road to pass to L of factory (it is on your R). Road climbs and when you are level with the last factory building fork R onto a track // to both road and electricity cables (between the two). *(You are now above and // to the river Arga in the valley below R.)*

Towards end of factory workings and at junction with another track coming from back R go downhill steeply (steps) following line of electricity cables. Cross road at bottom and KSO ahead. Cross stream and KSO down FP (// to and between two sets of electric cables) on paved path which then leads uphill between banks to emerge at side of house in hamlet of **Ilarriz** (2.6km). Turn L *(fountain)* and then R down minor tarred road. At bend in road (signed 'Eskirotz 500m') KSO(L) uphill to hamlet. Fork L at end along walled lane with fields below it to your R. KSO. Pass battery hen farm as track becomes unsurfaced road and KSO to minor (tarred) road. Cross it, go up short flight of steps and KSO on FP through field which continues alongside another and then between banks. Track climbs up and down, joined by another from back L shortly before you reach a minor road at entry to village of…

☗ 5.5km Larrasoaña (Larrasoaina) (53/725)

Fountain, bar/shop, bar/restaurant, *refugio* at side of town hall run by *alcalde*.
Village founded as a monastery, later donated to Leyre, formerly with pilgrim hospitals. Church contains statue of St James.

To enter village: turn R, cross bridge and then turn L at church. *To continue:* turn L onto road and follow it to hamlet of **Aquerreta** (1km, fountain). KSO(R) down green lane at house with armorial device (dated 1747). KSO downhill, cross minor tarred road (slightly staggered junction) and KSO ahead on lane. Track takes you in and out of woods above, but always // to, the main road below you to the R. Path then descends steeply (section with steps) to continue close to and // to river, passing weir (R) shortly before reaching modern bridge over the **Arga** at….

4.5km Zuriain 495m (57.5/720.5)

Cross bridge and veer L onto main road (N135). Continue along main road for 300m and then turn L down minor road (NA2339) signposted to 'Ilurdotz 3'. Recross bridge over the **Arga** (back on to the LH bank again) and take R turn at bend in road almost immediately afterwards. Continue on path to village of **Irotz** (2km). Veer R round side of large white house, pass in front of church (to your R) and KSO on concrete road. Cross medieval bridge back over the river again to village of **Uroz**. Turn L onto FP // to road (and between road and river). Continue to village of…

3km Zabaldica (60.5/717.5)

Church contains statue of St James but is usually kept locked so to see it you will have to ask for the key at a nearby house. (To visit it turn R in middle of tarred road for 20m and cross main road.)

Continue for 200m on FP on LH side of N135 then cross over to other side by picnic area just before road KM 9 and the old road bridge over the **Arga**. Fork R uphill up FP, track continuing high up but // to river below.

From here you can see the village of Huarte in the distance to your L and the Romanesque Ermita de la Virgen de la Nieve over on the hill on the opposite side of the river.

Continue to hamlet of **Arleta**, pass to RH side of church and KSO. KSO to dual carriageway, cross road by tunnel and veer R uphill on road on other side. This then veers L and leads, after a few hundred metres, to the bridge over the river **Ulzama** *(a tributary of the Arga)* at…

☗ 3.5km Trinidad de Arre (64/714)

Immediately after the bridge, on the R, is the Basilica de la Sanctísima Trinidad, with a small pilgrim hospital in former times and a *refugio* today run by the Padres Maristas.

Turn L after crossing the bridge *(fountain on R)* and enter…

0.5km Villava (Atarrabia) (64.5/713.5)

Suburb of Pamplona.

Bridge over the Ulzama at Trinidad de Arre (suburb of Pamplona)(Photo: Ysabel Halpin)

Go along main street for 1km past public garden (L) and bar (R) to cross roads with traffic lights. Continue straight ahead along a tree-lined *paseo (note elaborate Basque-style school of agriculture on R)* and enter suburb of...

1.5km Burlada (66/712)

Shops, etc.

When you reach some traffic lights with a garage (R) and the **Villa Josepha** with a large, tree-filled garden (L) *do not* continue straight ahead to cross the river by the road bridge; cross the road and turn R along the **Calle Larraizar** with a school on its R, past a block of flats, to the main road. Cross this and KSO on other side along a minor, tree-lined road (with garden centres on both corners), the **Camino** or **Carretera Burlada**, for 2km, ignoring LH fork at first 'kink' in road.

At a bend in the road you will get a good view of Pamplona cathedral and then note (L) two houses with façades decorated with scallop shells embedded in the stucco.

When you have almost reached the river *(fountain on R by school)* a minor road crosses the one you are on. Turn R and then almost immediately L over the **Puente de los Peregrinos,** *the old pilgrim bridge over the river Arga with a recently decapitated statue of St James on a small column at the far end.* Cross the public garden straight ahead towards the town walls, following waymarks, cross road at traffic lights diagonally R and KSO to walk between the inner and outer sets of ramparts. At the gateway KSO up the **Calle del Carmen** into the old quarter of...

🏠 3.5km Pamplona (Iruña) 415m (69.5/708.5)

Population 200,000. All facilities. RENFE, buses to Burguete, Puenta la Reina, Estella, Logroño. Tourist Office: Calle Anumada, near the Plaza del Castillo. *Refugio* (Easter–Oct only).

The end of the second stage of the *Camino de Santiago* in Aymery Picaud's guide. A fortress town situated on rising ground in the middle of a broad valley, Pamplona (Iruña in Basque) was the capital of the ancient kingdom of Navarre and is the capital of the modern autonomous region of the same name. It is probably most famous today for the festival of San Firmin during the first two weeks of July with the 'running of the bulls', but it also contains many places of interest (the Tourist Office produces a useful leaflet for a walking tour of the city) and it is worth spending at least half a day here. Gothic cathedral with

Pamplona cathedral, facade

outstanding cloisters, churches of San Sernin, San Domingo, San Nicolás and San Lorenzo. Museo de Navarra, Ciudadela (fortress area, now a park). Pamplona has many public fountains.

The route is waymarked through Pamplona with blue-and-yellow plaques bearing the Council of Europe's schematised 'path of the stars' motif (the direction to take is the one in which the 'point' of the cluster is facing.)

To visit the cathedral: turn off the **Calle del Carmen** at a small square with a statue.

To continue: KSO along the **Calle del Carmen**, turn R into the **Calle de Mercadores**, continue to the **Plaza Consistorial** *(with ayuntamiento)*, turn R into the **Calle San Saturnino** and KSO ahead to the **Calle Mayor** which then becomes the **Calle Bosquecillo**. At end, KSO, passing to L of a public garden. At the crossing of **Avenida Piu XII** and **Avenida Taconera/del ejercito** veer L to parkland surrounding the **Cuidadela** and follow the flagstone path (waymarked). When it turns in front of the **Cuidadela** veer R across the grass to the road. Cross this and continue down the **Calle Fuente de Hierro**, which leads downhill under the road bridge across the campus of the University of Navarre and then becomes the **Camino de Santiago.**

Continue ahead along a minor road signposted to 'Cizor Menor', crossing first the FB over the river **Sadar** and then the bridge over the river **Elorz**. KSO. When the modern road forks to the L, fork R, KSO and then go up steps in order to cross the railway track; then leave road off more steps on other side to rejoin path. Continue ahead. This path then becomes the pavement along the main road to the L, which it joins. KSO to top of the hill to the village of...

🏠 4.5km Cizor Menor 483m (74/704)

Bars, restaurant (but no shop), *farmacia*, fountain in public garden (R), *refugio*.

Restored Romanesque church of San Miguel on R of main road, remains of the 12th-century commandery of the Knights of St John of Jerusalem and the old pilgrim hospital on L. 12th-century church of Sanjuanista.

From here onwards there is very little shade.

Continue downhill on road and 100m later fork R down tree-lined FP down LH side of the *frontón* and veer L (KSO) to road which becomes track.

Ahead of you is the Monte del Perdón (1037m) and a line of 40 modern windmills along a ridge to its R, providing Pamplona with its electric power.

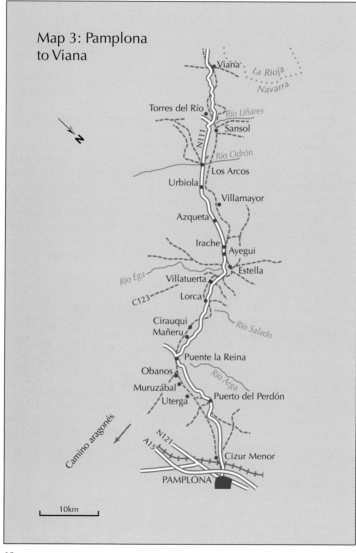

Map 3: Pamplona
to Viana

Viana

La Rioja

Navarra

Torres del Río

Río Liñares

Sansol

N111

Río Odrón

Los Arcos

Urbiola

Villamayor

Azqueta

Irache

Ayegui

Río Ega

Estella

Villatuerta

C123

Lorca

Río Salado

Cirauqui
Mañeru

Puente la Reina

Obanos

Río Arga

Muruzábal

Uterga

Puerto del Perdón

Camino aragonés

N121

A15

Cizur Menor

PAMPLONA

10km

The camino climbs beyond Pamplona (Photo: Paddy Dillon)

Join tarred road coming from L and KSO. About 100m later (road bends R) KSO(L) ahead on track. When this bends to R after 200m turn L up clear FP and then ridge through field. Go under both sets of electric cables and cross minor road. KSO on gravel track on other side. *Church and village of Guenduláin visible straight ahead of you on small hilltop.*

KSO, ignoring LH turn at junction by line of four large trees. Shortly before a group of eight trees track bends L: KSO(R) on earth track ahead. At junction with track *(small lake/reservoir to L)* turn L uphill. At next crossing 60m later KSO towards windmills on skyline. *(Good views of Pamplona to rear.)* Continue uphill to...

6km Zariguiegui 570m (80/698)
Fountain.

Continue straight on through village *(Romanesque church on R)* between houses and then ahead on a track (towards the windmills all the time). About 500m after village ignore L *turn* but take L *fork* at 'Y' junction 20m later, steeply uphill *(isolated tree on RH side of path near top is a good place for a rest from evening sun)*. KSO.

Splendid modern fountain (though not necessarily working) on your L (with seats) at a spot named **Gambellacos**. *Legend has it that a pilgrim making his way up to the Alto del Perdón, exhausted and overcome by a terrible thirst was accosted by*

Modern windmills on Alto de Perdón *(Photo: Ysabel Halpin)*

the devil, disguised as a walker, who offered to show him a hidden fountain but only on condition that he renounce God, the Virgin Mary and St James. The pilgrim refused but then St James himself, disguised as a pilgrim, led him to the hidden fountain and gave him water to drink in his scallop shell.

Reach the road at…

2.5km Alto del Perdón 780m (82.5/695.5)

Panoramic views ahead to Puente la Reina and laid out in front of you, like a map, are the villages you will pass through next: **Uterga, Muruzábal** and **Obanos**. At the crossing with the road there is now the 'Parque Eólico del Perdón', constructed in 1996, a picnic area with cast-iron 'cut-out' sculptures of pilgrims on foot and horseback, plus two donkeys and a dog. The inscription reads 'donde se cruza el camino del viento con el de las estrellas' ('where the path of the wind crosses that of the stars'), a reference to the *Camino de Santiago* and the Milky Way.

Cross over the road and go down the other side, watching out carefully for the waymarks, to valley bottom. Join track coming from back R and KSO(L). Cross small river (with a long line of trees along its bank) and go uphill again into village of…

Metal cut-out sculptures, plus real pilgrims, Monte del Perdón   (Photo: Ysabel Halpin)

🏠 3km Uterga (85.5/692.5)

Fountain, bar (unmarked), small simple *refugio*. Many fine old houses.

KSO through village, veering L, then take second RH turn onto minor road which becomes gravel lane, veering L downhill. At junction with crossing turn R onto grassy track between fields and follow it as it winds its way, mainly on the level, through fields to Muruzábal. Track becomes tarred and passes football field (on L), joining main road by village name boards in…

2.5km Murazábal (88/690)

Bar, fountain. Late 17th-century Palacio de Marquís de Zabalegui.

Go through village and as you are leaving it turn R diagonally, just before a large roadside cross (R), walking along the edges of fields. Join road coming from L and KSO. Fork R at top of hill into village of…

2km Obanos 414m (90/688)

Bank, restaurant, *panadería*, bar at end of village.

Ermita San Salvador, where the route from Roncesvalles is joined by the one coming from Arles over the Somport Pass. A short detour is recommended from here to the 12th-century church at **Eunate**, 3km away on the Monreal/Las Campanas road. It is an octagonal building surrounded by a series of arches and was used as a burial place for pilgrims.

Enter the village by the **Camino Roncesvalles.** KSO to **Calle San Juan**, turn R into the **Calle Julian Gayarre**, L down a tree-lined street with a school (L) to church *(public garden on its R)*. Continue diagonally through archway and KSO, following road as it bends to R passing *frontón (fountain opposite)* then the **Ermita San Salvador** (L). When the road becomes a rough track at the side of a farm (R), KSO above vines (to L) and follow it downhill to the main road.

Cross over and continue more or less // to it on FP alongside allotments. Rejoin road by hotel (on L).

Here there is a modern statue of a pilgrim to mark the junction of the caminos francés and aragonés.

Turn L along the N111 for 300m to…

Puente la Reina, pilgrim statue at junction of Arles and other routes coming from France

🏠 2km Puente la Reina (Gares) 346m (92/686)

Population 2000. All facilities. Buses to Estella, Logroño and Pamplona. Two *refugios*: one run by the Padres Reparadores, at entrance to town, one private (at exit). Hotel Yakue (at entrance to town) has pilgrim dormitory.

The town gets its name from the 11th-century pilgrim bridge over the river Arga. This was built at the command of Queen Urraca, daughter of Alfonso VI, and with its six arches remains unchanged today. It is also one of the most interesting on the *camino*. Church of Santiago (with statue of St James the pilgrim inside, on wall on left facing altar).

Turn L at *refugio, a two-storey building on the corner run by the Padres Reparadores, with an arcaded verandah outside*, and then turn R in front of the seminary, passing between it and the church (R). KSO down the **Calle Mayor** until you get to the old bridge over the **Arga.** Cross it and turn L on to road. Cross main road (near modern bridge) and fork L onto minor road, // to main road. When this veers R, back towards the main road, at large wayside cross *(picnic area, fountain)*, fork L onto unsurfaced road, which then becomes a cart track, running // to the river. Continue along it for 1.5km and then, 100m after sewage treatment plant, fork R uphill. Fork L shortly afterwards to a ravine and then follow track (now a FP) uphill again, turning R after a flight of steps onto a wide earth track leading steeply uphill. Pass site of former 13th-century **Monasterio de Bargota** *(fountain, picnic area and orientation plan on main road above to R)* and continue on track // to road until you enter village of…

5km Mañeru (97/681)

Bar, shop, *farmacia*, fountain.

Note medieval *crucero* (wayside cross) at entrance, moved when the road was widened.

Fork L down **Calle Mikelaldea**, veering R over bridge and continue to small plaza *(fountain)*. KSO ahead along the **Calle de la Esperanza** into the **Plaza de los Fueros** *(and the Casa Consistorial; note houses with* blazones). Cross it diagonally and then turn L and then R, to leave village via **Calle Forzosa/Camino de Santiago** and continue through fields. About 1km after Mañeru turn R along bigger track coming from L then KSO, in more or less a straight line all the time, ignoring turnings, to the hilltop village of…

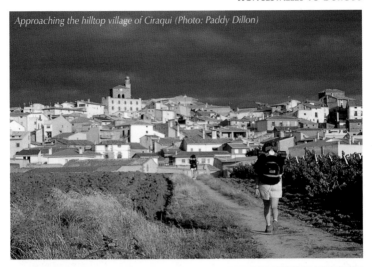
Approaching the hilltop village of Ciraqui (Photo: Paddy Dillon)

2.5km Cirauqui 498m (99.5/678.5)

Shop, bar, fountain in public garden. (Bar 100m to R on main road.)
Very well-restored ancient village with Gothic church of San Roman.

The route through Cirauqui is a bit complicated with all the turns indicated by the yellow arrows but, basically, you go round the base of the village in a clockwise direction and then continue the straight line you started on entering.

Turn R on street at entrance *(shop)* and then immediately L. KSO ahead (staggered) up unnamed street ahead under arch in tower and up to top of street (steep). Turn L at top into the **Plaza** and go *under* arch ahead *(with stone seats, a nice cool place to sit/rest)* and out the other side, turn L downhill and then R down **Calle del Mediodia**, second L downhill, veering R to join road coming from back L. This becomes a track. Follow it (tree-lined) downhill onto old paved Roman road which leads you over the river on the old bridge and continue till you reach the main road (N111) again, at a roundabout/turning area.

Cross the road, go up minor road and then turn first L onto earth road and KSO, ignoring any turns to R. Cross *old bridge (on site of former Gothic bridge and medieval route on line of Roman road)* and KSO. After 1.5km fork L along FP, cross gravel road by pylon, go down stone steps and continue on FP. When it widens out and bends L turn R, gradually descending to reach the road (N111)

69

shortly before a junction with a minor road to your R marked 'Monasterio de Alloz' and 'Embalse de Alloz' (a reservoir). Turn R on road, follow it under modern aqueduct and after houses on L turn L through two green gates onto a path which goes over an old bridge.

Roman bridge, Ciraqui
(Photo: Ysabel Halpin)

This bridge crosses the river **Salado** *('Salt River'), one of the many that Aymery Picaud warned pilgrims neither to drink themselves (nor allow their horses to), for they would die immediately. He also relates how he saw two Navarrese sitting there, sharpening their knives in preparation for flaying any pilgrims' horses who had the misfortune (as did his own) to drink from the river.*

Follow the path from the bridge and it will lead you *under* the modern road. On the other side turn R up an old road, fork L and follow it uphill to village of…

☗ 5.5km Lorca 483m (105/673)

Bar (unmarked, weekends only), fountain, rooms in house on main street, shop. Bar/restaurant Bodega Molino on main road.

Church of San Salvador, 12th and 16th centuries, with flamboyant Gothic cloisters.

Go through village past church (on R) and down main street to road. Continue along it uphill and at fork at top continue on small FP to LH side (to L of hedge) and KSO.

About 1km later turn L onto minor road which becomes an earth road and turn R at junction. KSO. Track joins from back L: KSO along it.

Around 200m before you reach a main road *(tunnels visible)* turn L, veering R, and go towards road. Go through tunnel, KSO and reach residential area in village of…

5km Villatuerta (110/668)

Two bars, *farmacia*, Ermita de San Roman, Iglesia de la Asunción (12th century onwards, with 15th-century frescoes).

Turn first L and KSO until you reach the **Plaza Mayor**, a newly laid-out square with *polideportivo (sports centre)* on L *(bar inside)*. Cross square diagonally, turn L down side of school and KSO to cross old bridge over river **Iranzu**. On other side turn L along **Calle Rúa Nuera**, passing through estate of new housing, past *Ayuntamiento* (on R, bar inside), uphill to church *(fountain with drinking water to rear of church)*.

Continue past church and at T-junction (of tarred roads) KSO ahead on grassy track between fields, veering R towards main road (N111). When you reach it continue on gravel *piste* on its LH side. Pass turning to the **Ermita de San Miguel** *(100m to L; this was originally a monastery belonging to Leyre, built in the 10th and 11th centuries but converted into an* ermita *in the 17th century).*

Continue on FP and reach road by a *merendero* (picnic area). Cross over, go down steps and KSO along FP, veering L and then R downhill to cross solid new FB over the river **Ega**. Continue straight ahead on other side, up earth road, passing to L of stone house (with brick window frames) opposite then continue downhill on other side of hill, passing factories and other industrial buildings. Reach a minor road (the earth road you were on becomes the **Calle de Candelitera**) and turn R along it *(turn left here for campsite)*.

Pass fountain (L, drinking water) opposite wayside cross (this is now the **Calle Curtidero**). Continue ahead, passing in front of the **Iglesia del Espiritu Santo** and below the church of **Santo Domingo** (now an old people's home). Go under main road and as you pass Roman bridge (on your R) street becomes **Calle de la Rúa/Rúa Kalea.** Pass the **Hospital de Peregrinos** *(refugio, on L at no 50)* and continue ahead past **Plaza San Martín** *(fountain and Tourist Office, both on R)* down **Calle San Nicolás** in...

🏛 4km Estella (Lizarra) 426m (114/664)

Population 13,000. All facilities, several *hostales*, buses to Pamplona, Puenta La Reina, Logroño. Tourist Office: Calle San Nicolás 3.

Estella (Lizarra in Basque) is the end of the third stage of the *camino* in Aymery Picaud's guide and contains several interesting Romanesque churches: San Pedro de la Rua, with very fine cloisters, San Miguel (now restored), San Juan Bautista, Santa María Jesús del Castillo, San Sepulcro. The Palacio de los Reyes de Navarra is a rare example of a secular Romanesque building, with some well-known capitals, including Roland and the Moorish giant Ferragut.

It is suggested that you obtain a walking tour leaflet from the Tourist Office to visit the town's many places of interest and proceed as follows to continue your journey.

To leave Estella carry straight on along **Calle San Nicolás** (behind Palacio). KSO and pass under archway at end of street to a road junction (church on your L). KSO along this (**Camino de Logroño**), which divides after 300m. Cross over to the RH side and take the R fork, up an earth road next to a petrol station (the **Camino de Estella**) and go uphill through waste land. KSO to village of...

2km Ayegui (116/662)

Just *before* you reach a square (**Plaza San Pelayo**, *houses, flats)* at the very top you can *either* a) turn L for the Monastery of Irache (visible ahead) *or* b) turn R to miss it. Both *caminos* join up again after the Hotel Irache (ahead on the main road).

Wine fountain in Irache (Photo: Paddy Dillon)

Turn L in square and then R downhill to road. Cross it and veer L up lane to the 12th-century church and **Monastery of Irache** (500m).

The Monastery of Irache was one of the first Benedictine houses in Navarre (it can be visited). It had a pilgrim hospice attached to it which was famous all along the pilgrim route. Fountain and shady picnic area, Museo del Vino.

Opposite the monastery an enterprising bodega (vintner) has installed a **fuente del vino** *(wine fountain), two taps with red wine, one with water, with instructions not to abuse the facility, offering pilgrims the opportunity to drink a glass and thus fortify themselves for the journey ahead. (Caution on hot days...) The message reads: '¡Peregrino! Si quieres llegar a Santiago con fuerza y vitalidad, de este gran vino echa un trago y brinda por la Felicidad' ('Pilgrim! If you want to reach Santiago strong and healthy, have a drink of this fine wine and raise a toast to Happiness').*

KSO ahead up lane. About 150m later turn R alongside houses to road opposite **Hotel Irache** *(bar/restaurant)*. Cross over and rejoin option b) behind it.

b) At the square *(flats, houses)* KSO ahead down very clear track (you can see it laid out well ahead of you) which veers R to reach minor road which passes the back of the **Hotel Irache** *(bar, restaurant)* on the main road. After the hotel (with road to your L), by a complex of wooden chalets, KSO ahead on earth track, go under the N111 and KSO in direction of pointed mountain ahead on the skyline all the time.

This next section is fairly shady and takes you along a gated track through undulating woodland.

73

KSO on clear track, ignoring turns.

Cross minor road and KSO on other side on similar track, passing white building (pump house). Go down fenced slope to wide earth road and turn R along it, gradually downhill. Turn L at next T-junction and go uphill to Azqueta, entering village via concrete slope. Turn R along main street, passing *fountain (and seats)*.

5km Azqueta (121/657)

Continue through village on road to junction with main road near tunnel (to back L). Fork R downhill to farm and turn L uphill behind last building onto earth track uphill through fields, later becoming a FP. When you emerge into a field of vines *(and tip of Villamayor church spire is visible ahead)* veer R along side of the field, uphill, turning L 100m later along field track, emerging from field to your R. Pass a restored building that looks like a double-arched church doorway but is in fact a medieval fountain and continue to village of…

♜ 2km Villamayor de Monjardín (123/655)
Iglesia San Andrés (12th–18th centuries). *Refugio* run by a Dutch evangelical group (Easter– end Oct).

Continue to church and turn L downhill, cutting down path to cut out zigzags. KSO a short distance and then turn R along a clear unsurfaced road leaving the one you are on (and which leads down to the main road ahead) at right angles. KSO, passing grove of trees and KSO ahead, passing stone shelter and statue on R.

The walking in the section between Villamayor and Los Arcos is easy (though watch out carefully for waymarks) and very pleasant in either very early morning or late evening light (remember to give yourself enough time to reach Los Arcos). There are no villages, no shade, no water, no roads and almost no buildings along the way; woods over to the L and, later, large rock formations ahead to R.

About 600m later reach tarred road (fountain). Cross over and KSO. At RH turn *after* the one with a barn to R turn R and then KSO(L) at fork 100m later by small ruined house. Around 500m later return to earth road (this was a short cut) and turn R, and 500m after that turn L onto track through fields, towards ridge of hills ahead. Follow it round to R, // to woods, and 1km later turn L at T-junction, just before ruined chapel on hill to L in front of you.

When track gets close to woods (on L) turn L onto smaller track. About 1km later KSO(L) onto earth track coming from back R (a short cut). KSO, ignoring LH turns at junction 300m later and KSO ahead, veering L, into the **Calle Mayor** in…

🏠 12km Los Arcos 447m (135/643)

Population 1500. Two *hostales* (one with restaurant), shop, banks, bars, bar/restaurant, pharmacy, post office, Tourist Office. *Refugio* in old school on R after crossing bridge outside town walls. Buses to Estella, Pamplona and Logroño. Fountain.

Now only a small town with an arcaded square but formerly very much larger. Church of Santa María with Gothic cloister and interesting choir stalls in flamboyant Gothic interior. Several houses with armorial devices on façades in the long Calle Mayor.

Continue down the full length of the **Calle Mayor** *(a very long street)* till you reach a small triangular 'square' at the bottom. Turn R into the **Plaza Santa Maria**. Pass church (on L) and go through archway ahead, cross road and then bridge over river **Odrón**, past *refugio* (R). KSO taking R fork uphill past cemetery (R), **Capilla de San Blas** (L), electricity substation (L) into open countryside. KSO.

From here you will be going more or less // to the road and on a clear, non-hazy day you will have a good view of Sansol 6km away in the distance. There is very little shade at all in this section but the walking is easy, through fields and vineyards, and is well waymarked.

Around 2.5km after Los Arcos turn R onto track by small square stone building and 50m later turn L onto track coming from R and then immediately fork R. KSO. KSO(L) at fork by bridge and turn L onto minor road (NA7205) at T-junction. KSO along it for 1.5km to…

7km Sansol 505m (142/636)

Small hilltop village with very few modern buildings. Food shop inside another one marked 'tabac' in main square.

This village gets its name from San Zoilo (the patron saint of its church, worth a visit, if it is open, for its frescoes of the Ascension and Gothic statue of San Pedro). Very good 'aerial view' of Torres del Rio from the forecourt in front of the church (and from where you can also see the path you will take to reach it).

After entry to village turn R into **Calle Mayor** (KSO if you want to visit church). Turn L into **Calle Real**, R into next street (uphill), next L, next R, next L and you will come out on the road again. Cross over (N111, KM68, *view of Torres del Río below you now, on a hilltop across the river Liñares*), go behind crash barrier and turn R down FP. Go under road, cross bridge over small river (probably dry, *fountain/lavadero on L)* and go uphill into village of…

> ⛪ **1km Torres del Río (143/635)**
>
> Private *refugio*, bar/restaurant, shop, bank (+CD).
>
> Another small village with very few modern buildings. 12th-century octagonal Romanesque church of Santo Sepulcro showing influence of Byzantine and Hispano-Arabic style (ask for key to visit). Fountain near second church.

KSO up street ahead, veering R, then turn L in front of **El Mesón** then cross small square *(shop to R)* and reach octagonal church. Turn L up hill *(bar/restaurant on L)* and either turn L for *refugio* or R to continue *(public phone on wall on L)*.

To leave village follow road uphill out through orchards and past cemetery (L) to open fields.

From here to Viana the camino plays 'hide and seek' with the N111 to short-cut its very many hairpin bends and thus goes in a fairly straight line, though climbing up and down a lot, into and out of valleys. Nice scenery on a clear day, with mountains in the background.

Go down into dip and up (twice) and KSO(R) at fork and continue on FP at edge of field, to LH side of road. Just below top of hill cross over and continue on FP on RH side, passing the **Sanctuario de Nuestra Señora del Poyo**. Shortly further on is an *ermita* (near Bargota). *Panoramic views from here, picnic area.*

Continue on FP. Return to N111 before a sharp hairpin bend at KM 72 and then turn R on FP uphill, forking L shortly afterwards. Reach road at top of hill – *first panoramic view of Viana and Logroño from here on a clear day.* Turn L and 100m later turn R onto RH of two tracks, veering L downhill to valley bottom. KSO(L) at T-junction part way down. Veer R and join wider track coming from R.

KSO(L) on wide earth road coming from back R then, when it bends R, KSO(L) ahead on track between vines. KSO(R) at fork and continue along valley bottom. At junction just past small house turn L. About 100m before you reach the N111 track but the track veers R but the *camino* continues uphill on FP to LH side of woods. Continue on it to road, cross over, and continue on FP on other side, to top of hill by bend in road.

Continue on road for 300m then continue on small FP to L, in field. Return to road for a while then take a small FP in field to LH side of road that brings you out opposite a huge grain silo on the outskirts of Viana. Turn L and fork R on other side on stony track. Cross a road, continue ahead (**Calle El Cristo**) past picnic area by house with large mural on its end and reach a 'stop' sign.

Cross first road and turn hard R up second. Cross **Calle Serapio Urra** at top, go through arch and turn first L into **Plaza del Coso**. Turn R along **Calle Santa María** into the **Plaza de los Fueros** and the church in...

🏠 11km Viana (154/624)

Population 3500. All facilities. Tourist Office, *hostal*, large *refugio* (Easter–end Oct).

Attractive small town with cobbled streets and a long association with pilgrims (there were formerly four hospitals). Church of Santa María (almost as grand as a cathedral), 15th and 16th century, mixture of styles, with the tomb of Cesar Borgia under the street in front of it. Numerous houses with armorial devices on their façades. The Parque San Pedro (behind remains of church of that name, *refugio* next to it) on part of the old town walls is a good place for a rest, with excellent views.

Leave Viana from the square in front of the church by the **Calle Navarro Villoslado**. Turn R in front of the ruined church of **San Pedro** *(façade interesting)*, R diagonally then L **(Calle San Felices)** under arch. R again (same street name) to the road. Cross it and take the second turn L down **Calle de la Rueda** then second R *(down street with tiny pilgrim in niche on house no 1)*. Turn L at bottom, cross road and then immediately fork R down street of new houses leading through allotments to a minor road (cross over) and then to the N111. Turn R here alongside it on a lane.

Reach N111 again, cross over and continue on track behind hedge to LH side of road before turning L, and then R, 200m later, on tarred road leading to the **Ermita de la Virgen de Cuevas** (1.2km).

This was once a chapel but is now a private house, by a stream, a shaded area with a lot of trees and picnic area, fountain with drinking water. (From here Logroño is visible ahead.)

KSO for 100m on tarred road then, at junction, KSO ahead on gravel track. Fork R 100m later towards barn and KSO in direction of main road.

About 1.5km later track veers L near wood. Turn R, go through wood, reach road, cross over and continue on FP on other side, through more woods, till you reach the **Papelería del Ebro,** a large factory on RH side of road. Cross FB over a small river and enter the province and autonomous region of La Rioja.

Continue on red tarmac lane to RH side of N111 which leads you under a tunnel under the main road 200m later, then under the motorway sliproad flyover, through another tunnel and then uphill through fields and downhill to the cemetery on the outskirts of Logroño 2km later.

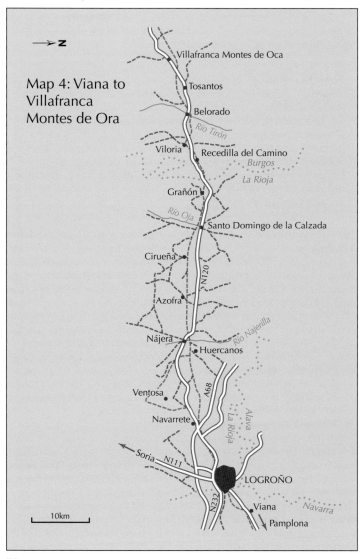

Map 4: Viana to Villafranca Montes de Ora

N

Villafranca Montes de Oca

Tosantos

Belorado

Rio Tirón

Viloria

Recedilla del Camino

Burgos

La Rioja

Grañón

Rio Oja

Santo Domingo de la Calzada

Cirueña

N120

Azofra

Nájera

Rio Najerilla

Huercanos

Ventosa

A68

Navarrete

La Rioja

Alava

Soria

N111

LOGROÑO

N232

Viana

Navarra

Pamplona

10km

Continue ahead along **Avenida de Mendavia** to the **Puente de Piedra** over the **Río Ebro**, turn L over it and enter...

🕮 9km Logroño (163/615)

Population 120,000. Large bustling city with all facilities. RENFE. Buses to Pamplona, Burgos, Madrid. Tourist Office: Calle Miguel Villanueva 10, large *refugio* in Calle de la Rua Vieja.

Cathedral of Santa María Redonda, with a carving of St James in the choir stalls and statue of San Roque at end of building inside. Church of Santiago has massive equestrian statue of Santiago Matamoros outside above south door and statue of St James on the altarpiece. Churches of San Bartolomé (interesting portal) and Santa María de Palacio. Logroño is a large town today but it owes its development to the pilgrim route, and the old quarter of the town is laid out along the line of the *camino*.

On the other side of the bridge take the second turn R down the **Calle de la Rua Vieja** (refugio *on L halfway along*), through the old quarter of the town, as its name suggests. At the end, continue along the **Calle de Barriocepa** to the **Fuente de los Peregrinos** in the **Plaza Santiago** (*with its modern chequered paving depicting sites along the route to Santiago on both the* caminos aragonés *and* francés – *in effect an outdoor board game*), and then to the church of **Santiago** *with its massive equestrian statue of Santiago Matamoros, St James the slayer of Moors, above the south door. (This is best viewed from a distance, down the Calle de Santiago opposite.)*

Continue along the **Calle de Barriocepa** to the end, where it bends round to the L, turn R, R again and then L under an arch in the old town walls. On the other side turn L and then immediately R **(Calle de los Depositos)** past a roundabout with *fountains (and tap)* to your L *(well waymarked)*. Cross a road L and then turn R down **Calle del Marques de Murieta**. Continue down this road for some time, past the Guardia Civil barracks. After crossing the railway line the road changes its name to **Avenida de Burgos.**

About 500m after this the waymarks indicate that you should fork L (**Calle Entrena**) behind a petrol station into an industrial estate. Turn L at end, then R between two factories before turning L again into the **Calle Prado Viejo**. However, it is much simpler to continue *past* the petrol station and then take the *next* LH turn into the **Calle Prado Viejo**. In either case, continue to end of this street and just before the *autovía* (dual carriageway) turn R onto a track leading down to a tunnel to cross this busy road.

Continue on other side on concrete *piste*, lined at intervals with recently planted trees. This is easy to follow and leads, after 1.5km, to some woods and a

Pantano de la Grajera between Logroño and Navarrete

tarred road just before the **Pantano de la Grajera** (a reservoir). At fork with fountain KSO(L) to edge of reservoir and then turn R along its retaining wall. Cross a bridge at the end and turn L under trees to cross FB over stream.

Veer R to pass behind *bar and picnic area* and then veer L along stony *camino* which leads you around the lake (though not along the water's edge) on gravel track. At T-junction turn R *(fountain)* onto tarmac lane. Turn L at next T-junction and follow track round to R, uphill, ignoring LH turns. This returns you to the main road *(view of lake and Logroño to rear)* at the turn-off to Navarrete after passing behind the petrol station and in front of a timber yard.

Take L fork at junction (N120) towards Navarrete *(up on hill ahead)*. After 200m cross road (carefully) and fork R down a track through vines and fields and cross a bridge over the motorway. To the L are the restored ruins of the church of the **Hospital de Peregrinos** of the *Order of San Juan de Acre, founded in 1185 to look after pilgrims.* Follow the track down to a farm immediately below another road. Turn L diagonally up some steps to this road, cross it and follow the street (**Calle de la Cruz**) into the village of…

☎ 13km Navarrete (176/602)

Population 1500. Shops, bars, restaurant, bank (+CD), Tourist Office. Several fountains. Campsite, *fonda*, hotel, *refugio*.

Navarrete has two *Calles Mayores, alta* and *baja* (both under restoration), arcaded and lined with *casas blasonadas*, houses with heraldic devices on their façades. The town also has several *alfarerías*, pottery factories and workshops producing goods in the dark-red clay seen everywhere in the landscape in this region. Monumental 16th-century church with a magnificent 17th-century Baroque reredos, gilded from floor to ceiling and wall to wall, with statue of St James near top.

Continue to church and then turn R and then L along **Calle Mayor Alta**. At end cross small square with fountain and turn L down **Calle Arrabal**. Continue on **Calle San Roque** and at a 'stop' sign KSO on N120 in direction of Nájera.

Pass cemetery (on L), *with 12th-century gates from the former hospital at the entrance to the village, installed there when the cemetery was established in 1875 (note two tiny pilgrims eating on capital and, on back of gates, carving of one weathered pilgrim with scrip and staff being force fed by another!). Outside it there is a monument to a Belgian pilgrim, Alice de Craemer, who was killed while riding a tandem to Santiago in 1986.*

KSO past cemetery and then leave road to continue on gravel track, at side of road to start with then further away, continuing ahead through vines.

From here to Nájera the manoeuvres may seem somewhat fiddly but they are designed to keep you off the N120 as much as possible, with its constant stream of juggernauts, cattle trucks, car transporters, ready-mix concrete lorries, huge vehicles laden with timber, clay, animals, and so on, as well as cars and buses doing 100kph...

At staggered junction 1.5km later turn R onto track leading to minor road by factory 300m later. Cross over and KSO on other side, then at T-junction of minor roads just before you reach the N120 turn R and then L along gravel track to its LH side, just before road KM 14.

When track turns away from road by area with seats (3.5km from Ventosa) turn R along earth track, // to N120. Turn R at junction by small building, return to road and KSO on LH side again.

About 300m later you can a) KSO on the road to go directly to Nájera (a total of 14km from Navarrete) or b) go via Ventosa, 2km longer, the hilltop village that you can see ahead of you to L. If you choose this option turn L, KSO and reach minor road at entrance to village.

🏠 **7km Ventosa (183/595)**
Refugio, 16th-century Church of San Saturnino, with splendid views all round on a clear day.

Poem on factory wall near Nájera (Photo: Ysabel Halpin)

To visit church and refugio turn L here. To continue to Nájera turn R then turn L onto earth track. (Small statue of St James the pilgrim on pillar at junction.)

Continue on track through vines (keeping straight on, R, at fork shortly afterwards). Join track coming from back R by small hut then another coming from back R. KSO(R) at fork.

When you go over the brow of the hill you will see Nájera in front of you. Descend gently downhill, passing to RH side of farm and reach lay-by on N120.

1.5km Alto de San Antón (184.5/593.5)

Ruins of a convent with pilgrim hospital.

Cross road extremely carefully and go down a flight of concrete steps on other side, then turn L onto earth track that continues below the road, undulating alongside fields.

The round hill that you see nearby is the Poyo Roldán, where Roland is reputed to have slain the Syrian giant Ferragut with a huge stone, in the same way that David killed Goliath (and from whom the giant is said to have been descended).

KSO(R) at fork. Reach minor road by gravel works and turn R, then fork L by factory buildings. Fork L to cross FB over dried-up **Río Yalde** (there is another memorial to Alice de Craemer here) then fork L through vines. Pass a huge factory (with a long pilgrim poem painted on its wall, in Castilian with a German translation).

Cross canal behind factory **(Canal Najerilla)** and KSO for 400m to minor road. Cross it and KSO on other side. At 'stop' sign KSO(R) ahead to a housing estate, passing a sports centre (R) and blocks of flats. KSO into street (bar and shop on

Polvo, barro, sol y lluvia
es Camino de Santiago.
Milláres de peregrinos
y más de millar de años.

Peregrino, ¿quién te llama?
¿Qué fuerza oculta te atrae?
Ni el Campo de las Estrellas
ni las grandes catedrales.

No es la brava Navarra
ni el vino de los riojanos
ni los mariscos gallegos
ni los campos castellanos.

Peregrino, ¿quién te llama?
¿Qué fuerza oculta te atrae?
Ni las gentes del camino
ni las costumbres rurales.

No es la história y la cultura
ni el gallo de la Calzada

ni el palacio de Gaudí
ni el castillo de Ponferrada.

Todo lo veo al pasar
y es gozo verlo todo
mas la voz que a mi me llama
la siento mucho más hondo.

La fuerza que a mi me empuja
La fuerza que a mi me atrae
no se explicarla ni yo.
¡Sólo el de Arriba lo sabe!

Dust, mud, sun and rain
is the road to Santiago.
Thousands of pilgrims
and more than a thousand years.

Pilgrim, who calls you?
What hidden force draws you?
Neither the Field of Stars
nor the great cathedrals.

It's not sturdy Navarre
nor the wine from La Rioja
nor Galician seafood
nor the fields of Castille.

Pilgrim, who calls you?
What hidden force draws you?
Neither the people along the way
nor country customs.

It's not history and culture
or the cockerel in Santo Domingo
de la Calzada
nor Gaudí's palace
nor the castle in Ponferrada.

I see it all as I pass along
and it is a joy to see,
but the voice that calls me,
I feel more deeply still.

The force that drives me
The force that draws me
I am unable to explain.
Only He Above knows!

E.G.B. (translated by the author)

R) and continue into the centre of town. Turn R near end to cross bridge over **Río Najerilla** in…

⚓ 7.5km Nájera (192/586)

Population 7000. All facilities, hotel, *hostal, fonda, refugio*.

End of the fourth stage of the *camino* in Aymery Picaud's guide. The town takes its name from the Arabic 'place between rocks', a name which will become more obvious as you leave the town along a track which wends its way uphill between high cliffs.

Monastery of Santa María la Real, containing royal pantheon and interesting choir stalls with pilgrim scenes and cloisters. Church of San Miguel (Antigua), Convento de Santa Elena, Church of Santa Cruz. The present bridge (1886) over the river Najerilla replaces the 12th-century bridge with seven arches built by San Juan de Ortega.

On the other side of the river follow the yellow arrows and turn R and then L, following the signs for the monastery. Cross a road, and turn L through archway **(Plaza la Estrella)** then R **(Calle de Esteban M de Villegas**, KSO on **Calle de los Martires** for church of Santa Cruz), then turn L **(Calle San Miguel)**. KSO ahead **(Plaza Santa María)** for *refugio* or, to continue, KSO ahead **(Calle de las Vuidas)** then turn R in front of monastery church, uphill **(Calle Costanilla)**.

However, for a shorter, more direct way, turn L immediately after crossing the bridge down the **Calle Mayor** *(pedestrianised), leading you to a triangular 'square' at the end, the* **Plaza España.** *Turn R here to the monastery church of* **Santa María** *(set into cliff at rear).*

Continue uphill into woods. About 800m later cross road by farm and KSO through vines; 300m later KSO(R) at fork.

About 1km later KSO and 150m after that reach minor road coming from back R. Turn L along it for 1.5km to the **Calle Mayor** in…

⚓ 6km Azofra 559m (198/580)

Village with two bar/restaurants, two shops, *farmacia*, fountain in main square. Two *refugios*.

Church of Nuestra Señora de los Angeles with sculptures of St Martin of Tours and Santiago as a pilgrim, with staff, cape and hat. Just outside the village on the R is the Fuente de los Romeros, near the site of a 12th-century pilgrim hospital with adjoining cemetery.

KSO down main street *(fountain on L in **Plaza de España**)* and continue to end of village. Turn R along main road for 150m then fork L onto farm road just after village name board and opposite **Fuente de los Romeros** (on RH side of road).

KSO through vines, ignoring turns to L and R and after 1km pass a *rollo (R), a medieval pilgrim cross.* When you reach a T-junction turn R and then L onto track // to the N120 over to your R.

Cross a minor road leading to San Millán de la Cogilla, near slip road to N120, and KSO through more vines and more fields.

The monasteries of **San Millán de la Cogilla** *– National Monuments – are definitely worth a visit but are situated 15km off the route to the south. The upper one, Suso, is Visigothic and contains the remains of San Millán, patron saint and protector of Castille. It dates from c.AD1000. The monumental lower monastery Yuso (it can only be visited on a guided tour) is mainly 16th–18th century. Both are closed on Mondays. There is no accomodation at San Millán but there is a fonda 5km away at Badarán, on the way back to the camino.*

Camino in La Rioja

The original camino ran in a straight line from Nájera to Santo Domingo de la Calzada, but today it is interrupted in three places by changes in land ownership. To avoid a long stretch on the main road an alternative route has now been waymarked and is easy to follow. It is slightly longer but has splendid views, taking you through undulating fields to the L of the village of Ciriñuela, passing by the edge of Cirueña.

Turn L at T-junction of tracks and KSO. KSO ahead at staggered junction 2km later, towards hills ahead. Continue, undulating, to outskirts of **Cirueña**. Turn R onto local road, pass entrance to **Ciriñuela** then 300m later turn L onto an earth road between fields. KSO along this for 3km, ignoring turns to L or R, until you reach the outskirts of **Santo Domingo de la Calzada**, entering the town opposite a sports ground on the main road. Turn L along it into the centre **(Avenida de Torrecilla en Cameros)** then KSO(R) down **Calle Doce de Mayo**, passing the **Casa del Santo**, *refugio, on R)* and the **Calle Mayor** to the cathedral in…

♨ 15km Santo Domingo de la Calzada (213/565)

Population 5000. All facilities, Tourist Office. Two *refugios* a) in Casa del Santo b) run by Cistercian nuns in Monasterio de la Encarnación, *hostales, fondas*.

The town takes its name from Santo Domingo (1019–1109). Originally a shepherd, he wanted to enter the monastery of San Millán de la Cogilla but was refused admission because he was illiterate. He then built a hermitage and chapel in a forest in a notoriously bandit-infested stretch of the *camino* between Logroño and Burgos and began to look after the needs of pilgrims. He built a hospital (today converted into a *parador*) and church in what became the present-day town, a causeway and bridge over the river Oja, and devoted the rest of his life to road and bridge building. One of his disciples, San Juan de Ortega, continued his work.

The town contains several places of interest (Convento de San Francisco, Ermita de Nuestra Señora de la Plaza, Cistercian monastery, ramparts and tower) but the most well known is the 17th-century cathedral of San Salvador, where Santo Domingo is buried. Look out for its two unusual occupants: a cock and a hen (both very much alive) in a cage high up inside the building, reminders of a miracle. A family of three pilgrims stayed in an inn in the town. The innkeeper's daughter is said to have made advances to the son, who refused the offer. In revenge she secretly placed a bag of money in his luggage and the following morning, after they had left, 'discovered' that the money had gone missing. The innkeeper pursued the family; the son was brought before the judge and condemned to death. The parents continued their pilgrimage to Santiago, but on the return journey spent the night in Santo Domingo de la Calzada once again.

The mother was not convinced that her son was dead. She went to the spot where he had been put to death and found him there, alive, though still hanging. Accordingly the parents went to see the judge to ask for their son to be released. Like his counterpart in the apochryphal account of the death of

Judas Iscariot he too was sitting at dinner when the couple arrived and, likewise, refused to believe them. He declared that the boy was no more likely to be alive than were the cock and the hen on his table to get up and fly – which they immediately did, as proof of the son's innocence.

KSO past the cathedral. Turn L at end of **Calle Mayor** and then R into **Calle de los Palmarejos** and KSO when it continues as **Avenida de la Rioja**. Cross the bridge over the **Río Oja** *(Ermita, 1917, at entrance to bridge)*.

On the other side turn R then *hard* L onto gravel road // to N120. Return to main road, cross over and fork L onto gravel road to RH side of ITV (vehicle testing station). At end turn L then R onto tarmac road and continue on tree-lined track on its LH side.

At crossing of similar tracks turn R then L onto another track // to road, gently uphill, passing large wayside cross **(Cruz de los Valientos)**.

About 1km later, by 'stop' sign, you can either a) KSO on road to Grañón (1.9km – take the RH option) or b) turn L on *camino* (3.2km), in effect going round three sides of a rectangle to avoid walking on the main road. If you choose this (longer) route turn R 200m later, passing bridge with seats.

About 1km later turn R at crossing *(with information board about Grañón)* towards main road. Just before you reach it turn L onto minor road (the two options join up here), leading uphill to road at 'stop' sign. Cross over, go up short flight of steps and continue up street ahead towards square and church in...

♜ 6.5km Grañón (219.5/558.5)

Shop, bakery, bar, pharmacy, *refugio* to rear of church.

Originally a walled town with two monasteries, a castle and a pilgrim hospital. 16th-century Ermita de los Judios.

Cross road on entering village, go up short flight of steps and walk along main street past church (L). Continue a little further and then turn R (waymarked). At first it may seem as though you are going back on yourself, but you then turn L by a modern barn building onto a minor road. Follow road round a bend after 200m (do *not* go straight on) to barn with yellow arrow on it. Cross bridge over **Río Relachigo** and take second L along farm road. Fork R after about 1km *(village of Recedilla del Camino visible ahead)* and follow track 1.5km to village. Just before you reach it turn R at farm to join road. Pass another *rollo* and *fountain* (R).

🏠 3.5km Recedilla del Camino (223/555)

Two bars (one with shop), bakery, *refugio*. Pilgrim information office at entrance to village (this is the start of the very long section of the *camino* through the autonomous region of Castilla-León).

Village with a long tradition of looking after pilgrims (there were formerly 3 pilgrim hospitals and 11 *ermitas* here), its single main street lined with houses bearing armorial devices. Church of the Virgen de la Calle (so named because her statue is outside the church, above the main door) contains a Romanesque baptismal font (worth examining in detail as all its sections are very slightly different) and a guide is often on duty here.

Between Grañón and Recedilla you pass from La Rioja into the province of Burgos.
    Continue along main street past church *(fountain)* and public garden *(fountain)* to end of village, reach N120 by its exit boards, cross over and continue on gravel *piste* to LH side of main road. KSO, turning L then R into...

🏠 2km Castildelgado (225/553)

Petrol station, bar/restaurant El Caserio and Hostal/Restaurante El Chocolatería (both on road) have rooms. Church, fountain.

KSO along **Calle El Cristo, Calle Mayor** and into the **Plaza Mayor**, passing both parish church and *ermita* and leave village via **Camino de la Cuesta**, downhill, to use a *piste* again, on LH side of road. Join minor road coming from R and KSO to village of...

2.5km Viloria de la Rioja (227.5/550.5)

Birthplace of Santo Domingo de la Calzada (1019–1109), who was born in house opposite church (which contains the font in which he was baptised).

Continue through village on main street, pass church and continue out at end, veering R, downhill, after which you continue on roadside *piste* again. KSO to...

🏠 3km Villamayor del Río (230.5/547.5)

Bar/restaurant. Fountain. (Despite its name this is not a 'big town on a river' but only a 'small village by a stream'.)

Continue through village on **Calle Mayor**, passing fountain. Pass to RH side of church and continue on *piste* again.

The walk in this section may not be very interesting but at least it is safe: pilgrims previously had to walk on the main road itself all the way from Recedilla to Belorado, with its fast, heavy traffic.

KSO ahead and at entrance to Belorado (1km from centre) opposite factory by town place-name boards cross road (*very* carefully) and fork R down track. Enter town via **Calle El Corro** to **church of Santa María** *(refugio adjoining)*.

⌂ 5.5km Belorado (236/542)

Small town with all facilities, population 2000, two *hostales, pensión, refugio*.
    Churches of Santa María (16th century, contains a Santiago chapel) and San Pedro (17th century) used alternately, summer and winter.

To go into town centre: turn L (church on R), L again and then R to arcaded main square. *Otherwise:* turn L in front of church but then turn R **(Calle Mayor)** then L **(Calle Raimondo de Miguel)**. Continue on **Calle Hipolito Lopez**, cross **Carretera de Haro** and KSO down **Avenida Camino de Santiago**. KSO and rejoin N120 by town exit boards.

    Cross over, pass to LH side of road and cross **Río Tirón** by pedestrian bridge (// to road bridge). Then turn L to continue on *piste* to LH side of road, passing petrol station (L). About 20m before KM 68 there is a turning to the L, down a minor road, signposted 'San Miguel de Pedroso 3': turn L here and then immediately R off it onto a track. Then, turn R again almost immediately and the lane you are on is now // to main road and remains so, more or less, to Espinosa del Camino.

    KSO, watching out carefully for waymarks. Cross a track and KSO along a grassy FP, joining a track from behind L and then another to side L. KSO and after 200m reach village of...

⌂ 5km Tosantos (241/537)

Bar 100m on main road. *Refugio* in former parish house. 12th-century Ermita Virgen de la Peña set into hillside on the R, on other side of main road.

Do not go as far as the main road but fork L uphill up a farm road. Follow this to the village of...

2km Villambistia (243/535)
Church of San Esteban, fountain.

Pass fountain and chapel of **San Roque** and *fork* (not turn) R **(Camino de Cozarro)** and continue on track through fields, // to road over to your R. About 1km later pass **Fuente de Cozarro** (*with picnic area*).

Continue on this track until you reach the road, turn L, cross over and fork R down gravel lane to...

1.5km Espinosa del Camino (244.5/533.5)

Reach small road *(bar on other side)* and cross over. KSO past *fountain* (R). Follow road round to R and then turn L behind the last line of houses onto a farm road. KSO, ignoring next three turns to R. Pass the **Abside de San Felices** *(ruins of the medieval monastery of San Félix de Oca, on R)* and continue ahead until you reach the road *(view of Villafranca Montes de Oca ahead, with its large, prominent church)*.

Fork R on FP through fields. Return to road, cross bridge over the **Río Oca** and enter the village of...

♔ 3.5km Villafranca Montes de Oca (248/530)
Bar/restaurant El Pajero has rooms, second bar does meals. Shop, pharmacy, *panadería*, fountain, basic *refugio* in former school to LH side of main street. A*campada* (tented *refugio*) in summer.

'Town of the Franks': like others along the *camino*, the village's name refers to the many Frankish settlers and traders who established themselves along the pilgrim route in the Middle Ages. Situated at the foot of the Montes de Oca it had its own bishop until AD1075 and an important pilgrim hospice as early as 884. This was superseded in 1380 by the 36-bed Hospital de San Antonio Abad, at present under restoration as a refuge. The 18th-century parish church of Santiago replaces an earlier building and contains a statue of St James.

Do not leave here late in the day and allow plenty of time. It is not difficult to find the way to San Juan de Ortega in good weather but it takes at least three hours and the route, at 1150m, is wooded and completely unpopulated. In this section the waymarks are the Council of Europe blue-and-yellow signs with the Milky Way logo.

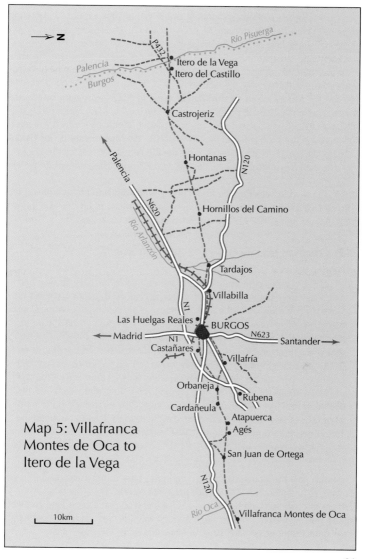

→ **N**

Río Pisuerga

P432

Palencia
Burgos

Itero de la Vega
Itero del Castillo

Castrojeriz

Palencia

Hontanas

N120

N620

Hornillos del Camino

Río Arlanzón

Tardajos

Villabilla

N1

Las Huelgas Reales

BURGOS

← Madrid   N1   N623   Santander →

Castañares

Villafría

Orbaneja

Rubena

Cardañuela

Atapuerca
Agés

San Juan de Ortega

N120

Map 5: Villafranca
Montes de Oca to
Itero de la Vega

Río Oca

Villafranca Montes de Oca

10km

Go along main street and fork R uphill behind the church (L), passing remains of **Hospital San Antonio** (R). Continue on FP, veering R to join track coming from back L. Take *second* L turn uphill and KSO. After 2km reach (signposted) the **Fuente de Mojapan** *(literally 'moisten bread,' a common pilgrim resting place in former times in an area too dangerous to cross at night and in which wolves were an expected hazard)*. KSO ahead.

KSO(L) at fork when terrain flattens out and KSO at crossing by fencing towards radio mast ahead. When track joins from back L, KSO. Main road gradually gets closer down below L and you are above it, shortly after which you reach the memorial to those killed in the Civil War (R), the **Monumento de los Caidos** (1163m). Descend steeply after this, cross the **Río Peroja** and then climb up again.

The path is in a dead straight line here, visible from the monument, // to main road below to L.

KSO on wide track coming from back L, with woods to LH side (this is the **Alto de La Pedraja**). KSO at crossings, ignoring turns to L and R, for 5km (6.5km from the war memorial). KSO(L) at a fork and KSO for 1.5km to…

☗ 12km San Juan de Ortega 1250m (260/518)

Refugio, bar, fountain.

Small hamlet with large pilgrim church of San Nicolás de Bari and monastery (recently restored), containing the elaborately decorated tomb of San Juan de Ortega ('St John of the Nettles'). After his ordination the saint went on a pilgrimage to the Holy Land and on his return set up shelter for pilgrims in the notoriously dangerous and bandit-infested Montes de Oca. One of the most famous architects of his day, San Juan de Ortega constructed the Romanesque church in such a way that at 5pm on the spring and autumn equinoxes (21 March and 22 September) – and only on those days – the rays of the setting sun light up the capital depicting the scene of the Annunciation. Instead of highlighting the angel Gabriel, as happens in most portrayals of this scene, it focuses on the Virgin Mary, thus transmitting the idea of fecundity and life. (The saint was also well known for his gift of making childless couples fertile.)

Continue past the church on road, veering L, pass minor road (to *Barrio de Colinas*, R) and then turn R onto wide track into woods.

Go through two cattle grids and KSO. When you reach open land continue ahead, passing well to L of *very* large wooden wayside cross and then go through small gate. Continue on earth road on other side down to village of…

Church at San Juan de Ortega (Photo: Ysabel Halpin)

3.5km Agés (263.5/514.5)
Sign indicating that there are now 518km to Santiago.

Path joins main street. Follow this past *fountain* (R) and follow street through village. Continue on road to...

☎ 2.5km Atapuerca (266/522)
Two fountains, two bars (one with resturant), *panadería, refugio*.
Fortress-like church uphill on R. Archaeological excavations in the late 20th century made a spectacular 'find': the fossilised prehistoric 'Atapuerca man'. Guided tours of the site are available, but it is 3km off the route.

Continue through village then turn L after second bar and bakery (both on R), uphill, veering L along line of fencing, to another very large wayside cross, at top. Continue ahead on open heathland, still following line of fencing then, as track becomes clearer and begins to descend, you have your first view of Burgos ahead.

KSO ahead, downhill or level all the time, passing quarry and group of antennae above it R. Reach earth road coming from quarry and turn L along it. About 300m later turn L down similar earth road, downhill. Near the end fork R and turn R onto minor road at entrance/exit to hamlet of...

93

4km Villaval (270/508)

KSO on road to village of…

2km Cardeñuela-Riopico (272/506)

KSO through village to end (bar) and continue on road to…

2km Orbaneja-Riopico (274/504)
Bar.

KSO. Cross motorway.

After this you have a choice of routes to enter Burgos (both of them way-marked). The historic route goes through Villafría but you then have 10km of main road with continuous fast, noisy, heavy traffic into the centre, the worst section of the entire camino (option A). Alternatively you can turn L here and take a slightly longer, definitely no more 'scenic' but quieter and much safer route to enter the town from the northeast, via the suburb of Castañares (option B). The two meet up before the centre of Burgos.

A: ROAD OPTION VIA VILLAFRIA
After crossing the motorway KSO along road for 2km till you reach the railway line (Madrid–Irún), // to it. Follow road round *(rubbish tip on L)* to cross bridge over the railway. Then: either follow road till it joins the N1 after 100m or turn R at bend in road immediately after bridge and go down lane to church of…

🏠 3km Villafría (277/501)
Now a suburb of Burgos. Two bars near church (whose tower has a complex arrangement of 'accommodation' for the storks), shop. Several bars on main road, *hostal*, bar with rooms, restaurant. Hourly bus service to Burgos Monday to Saturday but none on Sundays.

Turn L and continue on N1 towards Burgos, along the main road towards the city centre. After 4–5km and a large crossing the road becomes the **Calle Vitoria**. When you get to another large junction (traffic divides R for Santander, centre for city and L to Madrid) you can either continue along the **Calle Vitoria** into the centre of

Stork in 'residence', Villafría

Burgos or take a road // to it on the L, along the river and shaded, the **Avenida General Sanjurio**. This becomes the pedestrianised **Paseo de Espolón** in the city centre. Otherwise: turn R at the large junction along the **Avenida del General Vigón** and then L along the **Calle de las Calzadas** and *continue as described on page 97*.

95

B: ALTERNATIVE ROUTE VIA CASTAÑARES

After crossing the motorway turn L and pass in front of former military barracks and then turn R onto cart track through fields, which then give way to waste ground. About 1km later turn L at T-junction then R after another 150m.

Watch out carefully for the waymarks: with nowhere else to put them, these are often on the ground. If you lose them keep heading, in general, towards two large factory chimneys on the skyline ahead, one of them red and white and probably smoking, with the spire of Burgos cathedral behind them to their L.

About 500m later turn L at junction (by gate on R leading to airfield), veering R, then go under HT cables and pass tower, continuing to main road (N120) by fountain in…

3km Castañares
Bar/restaurant on main road.

Turn R down street just *before* you reach the main road, turn L and then R onto a *piste* alongside the N120. Cross slip road to N1 (Bilbao, Vitoria), go under bridge and cross another slip road, continue on *piste* and cross **Río Pico** *(probably dry)*. Around 200m after an *aparcamiento de camiones* (a huge lorry park) by exit board for Burgos, cross over to the other side of the N120 and go down lane opposite, veering R towards block of flats ahead. KSO along road ahead (**Calle Mayor de Villayuda**) and when tarmac stops KSO on gravel track alongside open ground (red-and-white chimney is now to your R). Track becomes the **Calle de Villafranca.** Go under railway line via a tunnel and go up steps on other side.

Here the yellow arrows fizzle out, but in the absence of any freshly painted ones proceed as described here (to join the route from Villafría and pick up the waymarks again).

Cross **Avenida del General Sanjurio** via pedestrian crossing, turn L and then R down some more steps and continue on **Calle de Villafranca** on other side. KSO along it and it continues again (to L) after a staggered crossing. At the very end *(bar, playground to R)*, by fountain, go down alley between walls, turn L then turn R down wide street, passing open-air swimming pool (on L) to **Plaza de Toros** *(bullring)* at end.

Turn R then immediately L down **Calle Plantio**, down RH side of **Estadio Municipal 'El Plantio'** (a football ground). Pass Red Cross hospital and then park; cross over and then cross the **Calle Vitoria** as well. Continue ahead on other side down **Calle Maestro Justo del Río**, a short street between the **Hôtel Puerta de Burgos** and the Guardia Civil barracks. Turn L, turn R (**Avenida de Cantabria**) then turn L to cross it opposite the beginning of the **Calle de las Calzadas** and continue down this street right to the end.

Cross **Plaza de San Juan** *(Museo Municipal on L, church on R)*, cross bridge over **Río Vena** and go through archway down **Calle San Juan**. Continue along **Calle de los Avellanos**, cross **Calle del Arco del Pilar** and continue down **Calle de Fernán González** at end to cathedral, passing to its RH side. *To visit:* turn L down steps to main entrance.

☎ 10km Burgos 856m (287/491)

Population 170,000. All facilities. RENFE. Buses to Pamplona Logroño, Madrid and so on. Tourist Office in the Calle de San Carlos. *Refugio* on *camino* on leaving town, in huts in park on other side of river near military hospital.

Capital of Castille and end of the fifth stage in Aymery Picaud's guide. A place to spend at least a whole day. Gothic cathedral with Santiago chapel, many other important buildings, including the Gothic church of San Nicolás and, just outside the town, the monastery of Las Huelgas with its church, very fine Romanesque cloisters, chapel of Santiago and museum and the Hospital del Rey for sick or tired pilgrims.

Burgos, Arco de Santa María

Burgos to León

To leave Burgos: from the cathedral (with the church of San Nicolas to your R) continue along **Calle Fernán González**, passing seminary (on your R), and go under archway at end. Turn L immediately down flight of steps, cross road and KSO ahead down **Calle del Emperador**, pass church of **San Pedro de la Fuente** *(L, fountain)* and turn L at the bottom into **Calle Vilalón**. Continue to end, bringing you to the **Río Arlanzón**, and cross it by the **Puente Malatos**.

Turn R on the other side along the main road past the **Hospital del Rey** *(now restored as part of the university's law faculty)* and the *refugio (in a park to L)*. After 3km, at traffic lights opposite a restaurant, the main road veers L. Fork R down a minor road (tree-lined). At the end (0.5km) KSO along a farm track (// to railway line to L) past fields, a tree plantation and more fields. KSO ignoring turns to L and R. After another 3km reach…

♨ 5km Villabilla de Burgos 837m (292/486)
Bar/restaurant, small basic *refugio*. Church (L) on other side of railway line.

Cross minor/branch line but *not the main (Madrid–Irún) line. Fork R, passing to the L of a house in front of a flour factory (R). Follow the road round to the R, cross a bridge over a river and turn L on other side, past two bridges on to a farm road through fields. (Main road ahead to L.)* KSO for 1km till you reach the road. Turn L along it, cross to other side, and cross bridge over the **Río Arlanzón.**

After bridge fork L down a track // to main road and continue on it until it joins the road at entry to…

♨ 4km Tardajos 828m (296/482)
Shops, bars, restaurant (with rooms), *fonda, refugio*.

Pass *rollo* on L on entry. Fork L opposite bar down **Calle del Mediodía**. Turn R at end and then L on to a minor road. Cross **Río Urbel** and KSO to…

1.5km Rabé de las Calzadas (297.5/480.5)
Fountain.

Winding path through the meseta near Hornillos (Photo: Paddy Dillon)

KSO through village and turn R in a triangular 'square'. KSO. Fork R at modern chapel (L) by cemetery (L) then fork L 50m further on.

Track joins from R 3km later and the path levels out to a vast, seemingly endless plateau. KSO.

This plateau is the meseta, lush and green in spring, a dustbowl in summer. You will either find it extremely tedious or, if you like undulating expanses reaching out to infinity in all directions, hauntingly beautiful, especially in the early morning light. Although it is so far removed from the noise of 'civilisation' it is, in fact, far from silent; you will soon be aware of just how much sound is produced by the wind, insects, birds and grass.

Path descends to a valley, then some 1.5km before the village ahead join unsurfaced road coming from R. When you get to a road cross it and enter village of...

🏠 8km Hornillos del Camino (305.5/472.5)

Refugio, bar (does meals).

Small village with a large Gothic church, formerly an important pilgrim halt with a hospital and a small Benedictine monastery.

Continue to the end of the village and turn R at the public weighbridge. Turn L after 1km and fork R (keep straight on) 500m further on. Fork R again after 10m, uphill all the time. Turn L at next junction.

At the top of the hill and beginning of the plateau cross a track and KSO.

Apart from electricity pylons in the distance to the L there is no sign of any sort of habitation in any direction, giving a feeling of being on the 'roof of the world'.

KSO at next two junctions (first is a crossroads, second a T-junction to L) and continue to the isolated...

🏠 6.5km Arroyo San Bol (312/466)

In medieval times there was a small hamlet here, San Baudilio, with a leper colony during the 14th and 15th centuries and a hospital, known as San Boal, set up by the Antonin monks from Castrojeríz to tend to sick pilgrims. There was also known to have been a settlement of Sephardic Jews here but the hamlet was mysteriously abandoned in 1503 and there is no trace of it left today.

About 100m off the camino to the L is a spring, reputed to have medicinal properties, with a small, simple refugio (April–Oct) in the building beside it.

Pass the turning to the spring and KSO. Shortly afterwards track descends to valley. Keep R at fork. Cross another unsurfaced track (ruined houses to L and R)

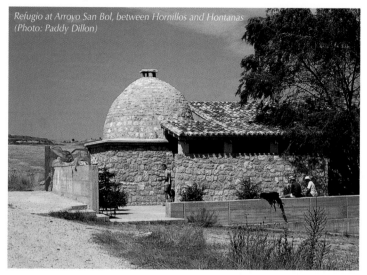

Refugio at Arroyo San Bol, between Hornillos and Hontanas (Photo: Paddy Dillon)

and KSO uphill again. Turn L at next fork (straight on) and the path levels out again. *Nothing in sight for miles and miles around.*

Cross a minor road and KSO *(two large clumps of trees away to R in distance)*. Cross grassy track and KSO. Cross another track and KSO again.

About 2km past the last minor road a valley suddenly appears on your R. KSO. Around 500m later another valley appears ahead and just after that another path joins from behind L. Then – all of a sudden – the church and village of **Hontanas** appear below you. Go down the path into the village, following the path to the R and then to the L down the main street in…

☎ 5km Hontanas 870m (317/461)

Fountain, bar (meals), swimming pool with bar (summer), two *refugios* (one municipal, closed in winter, one private).

Pilgrim village (its name means 'the fountains') dominated by its church.

Continue past fountain (L), church (L), weighbridge (R) and swimming pool (R). When you get to the road the waymarks direct you to cross it and fork R (that is, to L before you've crossed over) along a track on the other side. Although this takes you off the road, // to it, there is hardly any shade and you

Church in Hontanas (Photo: Ysabel Halpin)

may prefer to stay on the road as it has very little traffic and is tree-lined almost all the way to Castrojeriz.

Otherwise, after crossing the road, turn L 300m further on, at a junction after three large trees. When you reach the ruins of the **Molino del Cubo** take the upper path (keep your height) and KSO, uphill slightly, to the ruin of **San Miguel**. Pass below it. The track then descends to join another from the R. Fork L. About 10m later a track joins from behind L – KSO (still // to road). KSO at next fork. Track then veers L to join road. Follow it for 1km to the ruins of...

6km Hospital San Antón (323/455)

Gothic hospital founded by the Antonins, the French order believed to possess powers of healing St Anthony's Fire (a type of gangrene which appeared in Europe in the 10th century). Pilgrims who have come along the route from Le Puy will already have encountered this in the village of Saint-Antoine. Pilgrims came here in search of a cure and were sent on their way after a blessing with the 'Tau' (T-shaped) cross. The remains of the hospital are on both sides of the road, which passes under an archway. Bread for pilgrims was placed in a niche to be seen on the left of the road.

Continue along tree-lined road *(ruins of alcázar on hill above town visible ahead)* to...

⌂ 4km Castrojeriz 800m (327/451)

Population 1185. Shops, bars, restaurant, bank. Two *hostales, refugio* right at end of village, campsite.

Town built by the Romans and an important stopping place for pilgrims in former times: there were still seven hospitals left at the beginning of the 19th century. Collegiate church of Nuestra Señora del Manzano (13th and

Colegiata de Nuestra Señora del Manzano and hilltop castle, Castrojeriz (Photo: Paddy Dillon)

17th centuries, with statue of St James), church of San Juan (interesting cloister), church of San Domingo (with small museum).

Turn R at entrance to Castrojeriz to church of **Nuestra Señora del Manzano** *(worth a visit)* and then turn L through village (very long). To leave, pass church of **San Juan** (R) and go down to road. Veer L to crossroads. Turn L, cross road and after 50m turn L down an unsurfaced road. After 1.5km cross bridge over **Río Odrilla** and shortly afterwards *(house visible away to L)*, at staggered junction, KSO up path that winds its way, veering L, up to the top of the hill and the monument you can see on the skyline: this is the **Alto de Mostelares**. You are back on the *meseta* again (1km from bridge). At the top KSO (don't turn L) towards iron crosses (waymarks).

KSO, following the waymarks *(crosses with yellow plastic on them)* and shortly afterwards, after about 500m, you look down to a huge valley (bowl-like) below you. *Panoramic views.* From here the path leads more or less straight ahead to **Itero del Castillo** (though it doesn't actually go into the village).

Descend on track through fields for 1–2km. Cross a farm road and KSO. Fork L slightly downhill when track divides. Cross another farm road and KSO and about 1km afterwards join a minor road, going slightly uphill, at the **Fuente del Piojo** *(fountain and picnic area)*.

Turn R along road for 1km to crossroads. *(Itero de la Vega visible ahead.)* Turn L along road (ignore farm track back to L). Pass 13th-century **Ermita San Nicolas** (L).

The Ermita San Nicholas was a former pilgrim hospital which has now been converted into a small refugio *by the Confraternita dei San Jacopo, the Italian association of the Friends of St James), who open it from June to September.*

Cross bridge over **Río Piserga** – the boundary between the provinces of Burgos and Palencia. *(The 65km stretch of the* camino *which passes through Palencia is particularly rich in historic monuments.)*

Fork R on other side of bridge down minor road for 1.5km to village of…

♻ 11km Itero de la Vega (338/440)

Two shops, bar (meals by arrangement), *refugio* next to *Ayuntamiento*.

13th-century Ermita de la Piedad (with statue of St James the pilgrim) at entrance to village, 16th-century church of San Pedro.

KSO through village **(Calle Conde Vallellano, Calle Santa María)**, cross end of main square *(fountain,* rollo). Continue straight on and then turn L down **Calle Marqués**

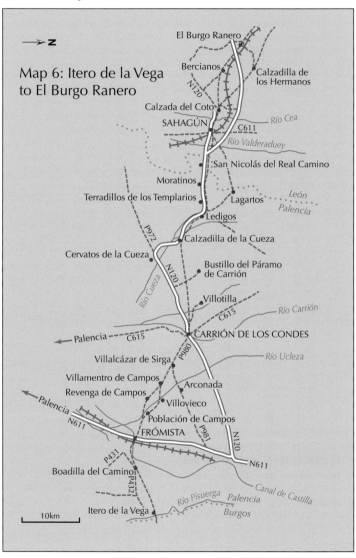

→ N

Map 6: Itero de la Vega
to El Burgo Ranero

El Burgo Ranero

Bercianos

Calzadilla de
los Hermanos

N120

Calzada del Coto

SAHAGÚN

Río Cea

C611

Río Valderaduey

San Nicolás del Real Camino

Moratinos

Terradillos de los Templarios

Lagartos

León
Palencia

Ledigos

P972

Calzadilla de la Cueza

Cervatos de la Cueza

N120

Bustillo del Páramo
de Carrión

Río Cueza

Villotilla

C615

Río Carrión

←Palencia— C615

CARRIÓN DE LOS CONDES

P980

Villalcázar de Sirga

Río Ucleza

Villamentro de Campos

Arconada

Revenga de Campos

Villovieco

←Palencia

N611

Población de Campos

P981

N120

FRÓMISTA

N611

P431

Boadilla del Camino

P432

Canal de Castilla

Río Pisuerga

Palencia

Burgos

10km

Itero de la Vega

de Estrella, following white arrows painted on road. Turn R into **Calle Comandante Ramirez.** Pass five large trees (L) *(another fountain)* and KSO to crossroads.

Cross road and continue along track flanked by water channels on either side. Pass turning (L) to hamlet of **Bodegas** after 1km and KSO. Cross bridge over **Canal del Pisuerga** and continue straight on to top of hill *(three humps visible ahead on skyline). View of Boadilla del Camino (3km ahead) at the top.*

Cross canal and turn R along bank. Then either follow street round to R to leave village or head for church to enter it. [RJ: fork R at fountain.]

♙ 8km Boadilla del Camino 782m (346/432)

Bar/restaurant has private *refugio* (small shop next door).

Church of Santa María has Romanesque font, the only one of three churches (and two pilgrim hospitals) that originally existed in this village. 15th-century *rollo*.

To leave continue past bar and then turn L alongside football ground (R) and L again past warehouse along unsurfaced road. KSO. Go through a gap in the irrigation channels (raised up) and 200m further on fork R up a bank to join the towpath of the **Canal de Castilla**. KSO along it for 3km. Cross the footbridge over the canal by a lock, veer R down a FP down a bank, go along a tree-lined path for 100m and turn R onto road. Follow it, veering L under railway bridge to crossroads (by *Tourist Office*). [RJ: follow signs for 'Astadillo' to bend in road (to R) and then cross canal at footbridge.]

♙ 6km Frómista 780m (352/426)

Population 1400. All facilities. RENFE. Hotel, *hostal,* two *pensiones*, *refugio* opposite church in Calle del Hospital.

End of the sixth stage in Aymery Picaud's guide. Small town with Romanesque church of San Martín (now deconsecrated), a National Monument and one of the most well preserved of the whole *camino*. It has a frieze of 315 carved figures of animals, humans (some humorous), flowers, monsters and so on round the church under the eaves, all in perfect condition. Church of Santa María del Castillo (also a National Monument), erected on the site of an ancient fortress, has an altarpiece with 29 paintings. 15th-century church of San Pedro, Ermita del Otero.

To leave: KSO along road to Carrión de los Condes (cross road at crossroads by Tourist Office).

Romanesque church of San Martín, Frómista   (Photo: Paddy Dillon)

*The new route takes you alongside this road on a specially prepared andadero de peregrinos, running parallel to it like a cycle track all the way to Carrión de los Condes. It passes the entrances to **Población de Campos** (bar, refugio) and **Villovieco**, goes through **Villarmentero de Campos** and **Revenga de Campos** (bar) and past the entrance to **Villalcázar de Sirga**.*

Alternatively, you can continue on the old route, turning R after 4km on the road into...

🏠 4km Población de Campos 790m (356/422)

Two bars (one does meals), shop (unmarked), very small *refugio.*

Small village with the remains of a former pilgrim hospital. 13th-century Ermita del Socorro, Ermita de San Miguel, 17th-century church of the Magdelena, Fuente San Miguel L near cemetery.

Fork R up concrete road **(Paseo del Cementerio)** to visit village, aiming for church. At junction behind church take minor road ahead with raised irrigation channel down LH side. KSO. After 3km pass a *fountain on RH side, built in 1989, with a wayside cross, shell and red/white cross motif.* KSO to...

4km Villovieco 790m (360/418)

Turn L over bridge over the **Río Ucieza** and then immediately R along its bank and KSO. Follow the bank for 5km, as far as the **Ermita de la Virgen del Río** *(contains alabaster statue of St James the pilgrim)*. Sometimes it is necessary to cross small irrigation channels running at right angles to the river – some have stepping stones – and then go back onto the path again. The last 1km is fairly shady.

Turn L along the road when you reach the *ermita (a large building, similar to a church but now a private house)* which is near a bridge. Then pass the **Ermita del Cristo de la Salud** *(small – still in use)* (L) and after 1km enter…

⌂ 6km Villalcázar de Sirga 809m (366/412)

Bar, two shops, restaurant, two *hostales*, *refugio*, fountain in public garden.

Also known as 'Villasirga', the village is dominated by the 13th-century church of Santa María la Blanca, a National Monument, with very fine portals, chapel of Santiago with tombs and statues, including one of St James, all in a very fine state of preservation and well worth a visit.

Turn R to enter village. Otherwise KSO to main road. Turn R and continue along it on an *andadero*.

Cornfields to both sides in an undulating landscape with bodegas *in fields to side of road. No shade at all*. KSO to…

⌂ 6km Carrión de los Condes 840m (372/406)

Population 2800. All facilities. *Refugio* near church, private *refugio* in Convento de Santa Clara (entrance to town). Campsite near river.

Formerly a large town with 12,000 inhabitants, 12 churches and several pilgrim hospitals, this is only a small place today, animated solely by the passage of pilgrims. Churches of Santa María del Camino (or de la Victoria), Santiago (splendid portal, church burnt in 1809 War of Independence, museum of religious art inside), Monastery of San Zoilo (National Monument, now a luxury hotel) with 16th-century cloisters, Convento de Santa Clara and museum.

Make sure you take enough food and water with you before you leave Carrión de los Condes.

To enter town: turn L off road at flour factory and KSO to square and church of **Santa María**. *To leave:* continue ahead here and turn R. Pass in front of church

109

Kilometre marker near Carrión de los Condes
(Photo: Paddy Dillon)

of **Santiago** and veer L to cross the **Río Carrión** by the main bridge.

Apart from a 'kink' by the Abadía de Benvívere the camino goes – quite literally – in a straight line until it reaches Calzadilla de la Cueza.

Pass in front of the **Monasterio de San Zoilo** (L) and come to a large crossroads 300m later. KSO for 300m further, past a petrol station, to another crossroads where the N120 veers L. KSO along a minor road which is signposted to 'Villotilla 6'. KSO for 4km.

Pass the **Abadía de Benvívere** (R), *former abbey but now a private house,* just before a sharp bend in the road where a bridge crosses a small river. About 300m after the bridge there is a junction with a minor road: cross it and KSO along a farm road through cornfields. *The landscape is flat in all directions.*

KSO for 2.5km to plantation of *chopos* (poplars, R) and road. Cross it, KSO for 6km, ignoring turnings to L and R. The church tower and cemetery are visible to the R shortly before you enter the village of...

🏠 17km Calzadilla de la Cueza (389/389)

Hostal/restaurant, refugio. Shaded area with seats at end of village (R).

Continue straight on through village to road. Cross the **Río Cueza** and KSO on the road, passing the remains of the *11th-century pilgrim hospital, formerly very important,* of...

2km Santa María de las Tiendas (391/387)

There are plans to restore this building as a refugio. *From here the landscape becomes less flat and slightly undulating. Woods to L and R, away from road. Mountains in distance to R. This is roughly the halfway point on the Spanish section of the* camino, *three-quarters of the way to Santiago if you started in Le Puy.*

Continue on main road to…

⌂ 4km Ledigos 883m (395/383)
Small bar/shop, private *refugio*. Church of Santiago with three statues of St James.

At entrance to village fork L off road and continue on track through fields, turning R 300m later, then L 500m after that. At junction 1.5km later turn R and continue to…

⌂ 3km Terradillos de los Templarios (398/380)
Shop, private *refugio*.
    As its name indicates, the village was originally owned by the Knights Templars, under the patronage of those in Villalcázar de Sirga. 18th-century church of San Pedro.

Continue out of village on track veering L onto minor road then turn R through fields, // to main road, crossing the two parts of the **Arroyo de Templarios**. KSO to…

3km Moratinos (401/377)

Continue along **Calle Real** past church and continue ahead, through more fields, veering R and then L into…

2.5km San Nicolás del Real Camino (403.4/374.5)
Brick church in Mudéjar style, fountain.

Continue through village, turning R and then L to cross the **Río Sequillo** and a road. KSO at junction 1.5km after village and leave the province of Palencia to

111

Sunlit cornfield (Photo: Ysabel Halpin)

enter that of León. *Sahagún is now visible ahead.* Turn R to return to road just before bridge over the **Río Valderaduey**.

Turn L along it then almost immediately R onto track on LH side of river, then turn L 600m later by the **Ermita Virgen del Puente** *(trees, picnic area)*.

This was formerly a pilgrim hospice and the path leading from here into Sahagún is still known as the Camino Francés de la Virgen.

Follow the path ahead, veering L, and 1km later go under the main road. KSO on other side, aiming for a very large white grain silo ahead. When you get there, cross the N120 and enter…

☎ 7.5km Sahagún 816m (411/367)

Population 2700. All facilities. RENFE on León–Palencia line, *refugio* in upper part of the Iglesia de la Trinidad. Convent of the Madres Benedictinas also has rooms (often full July–August). Campsite, swimming pool. Tourist Office.

End of the seventh stage in Aymery Picaud's guide. Sahagún takes its name from a contraction of San Fagún or Facondo, a Roman martyr. A monastery was founded here as early as AD904 and then, in 1080, the order of Cluny established itself and Sahagún became the foremost Benedictine abbey in Spain. Nothing remains of the original buildings (apart from a large gateway and belfry in the centre of town), nor of the five pilgrim hospitals founded in the 11th

New marker stone near Sahagún (Photo: Paddy Dillon)

century. But there are several churches of outstanding architectural merit: San Tirso, San Lorenzo and La Peregrina (all three National Monuments), San Juan de Sahagún, La Trinidad and, 5km to the south, San Pedro de las Dueñas (also a National Monument).

After crossing the main road continue down a small street (**Calle Ronda Estación**). As you approach the railway line (with the station on your L) follow it for a short distance and then cross it at the bridge. KSO down the **Calle José Antonio**, the **Calle del Peso** (fork R after this for the town centre), the **Calle Rua** and the **Calle de las Monjas.** At the end you will come to an open space, with the **Convento de las Madres Benedictinas** and the museum of religious painting on your R. (Turn R here for the *Arco de San Benito* and the church of *San Tirso*).

*To leave Sahagún continue straight from the **Calle de las Monjas** along the **Calle de Rey Don Antonio** and out of the town across the bridge over the **Río Cea**.*

This river is bordered with poplar trees, and legend has it that at a time when both Moors and Christians were battling for control of northern Spain a Christian force camped near Sahagún. Before retiring for the night some of the men stuck their lances in the ground and woke up the following morning to find that they had sprouted roots, branches and leaves.

Pass the swimming pool (R) and follow the main road to León to...

🚶 4.5km Calzada del Coto (415.5/362.5)

Two shops, bar, basic *refugio*.

Leave the road here along a turning to the R.

At this point the camino divides, the two paths running more or less parallel to each other with the railway line in between for much of the way, merging when they reach Mansilla de las Mulas.

A: CALZADA DE LOS PEREGRINOS

This is an old Roman road, the Vía Trajana, but is very isolated and there is virtually no shade for 30km. It is definitely not recommended in July or August; but for fit walkers who like space, silence and solitude it is perhaps the more attractive of the two routes at other times, provided you carry plenty of food and water and set out very early in the morning if you intend to go all the way to Mansilla de las Mulas. There are not many waymarks on this route but it is easy to follow as there are few turnings to make and, like most of the rest of the camino, you are always walking in a straight line due west.

After turning R into the village of **Calzada del Coto** pass the **Ermita de San Roque** on your R, cross over the motorway and follow the street through the village. At the end ignore the track to the L *(this leads to Bercianos)* and KSO(R). After 2km cross the bridge over the railway line *(artificial lake to L on other side)* and KSO.

After this you enter a wooded area, going gradually uphill. *Small, scrubby trees and a little shade.* After 3km (from the railway bridge) and just before you leave the woods, pass the **Granja Valdelocajos**, a large farm with modern houses and (some very large dogs). About 1km further on, on your R, is the **Fuente de los Peregrinos** and a picnic area. KSO for 3km till you reach...

☗ 12km Calzadilla de los Hermanillos
Two bars, shop, *refugio*, fountain.

Enter the village and KSO along the main street, past the *ermita* (L) and continue to the end where a road joins from behind R.

Continue on the road across an immense plateau stretching to the horizon on all sides. *From time to time you can see the poles along the railway line away to the L and the grain silo at El Burgo Ranero, and you may see/hear a train in the distance, but otherwise all you can see around you are the cornfields, seemingly reaching away to infinity.*

After 3.5km you will come to a junction where the *camino* ceases to be tarred and continues as an unsurfaced road, on the other side of the tarred road that crosses it *(L to El Burgo Ranero, R to Villamartín de D. Sancho)*. KSO for 13.5km, ignoring any turnings you may see to L and R, until you reach the deserted railway station *(apeadero,* 'halt, stopping place') at...

17km Apeadero Villamarco
Trains do still stop here, though only on request.

Do not cross the railway line at the station *(the road on the other side leads to the village of Villamarco, some 2km to the south)* but KSO more or less // to it. After 4km you will pass through the valleys of two dried-up rivers and from time to time you will see tracks leading off to L and R. KSO. After a further 6km you will enter two more river valleys – the path veers L here: follow it and KSO. About 200m after emerging from the second valley there is a junction: KSO and the church tower of **Reliegos** is suddenly visible ahead.

If you want to go there (bar, refugio*) and finish by the* Camino Real Francés *KSO (you are about 500m away from it).*

Otherwise: turn R down a track shortly after the junction. Go downhill along a track in a straight line for 6km until you reach **Mansilla de las Mulas** *(and which you will have seen ahead in the distance since nearing Reliegos).*

Enter the town by a canal and turn L along the main road. KSO at junction, enter town and KSO along main street *(see page 119).*

B: CAMINO REAL FRANCES
This route passes to the south of the other one, though leading directly west. Much of it has now become like a cycle track, initially prepared for the 'invasion' in the 1993 Holy Year. It is tree lined on one (the sunny) side only and has picnic areas at intervals.

At the point where you turn off the main road from Sahagún towards **Calzado del Coto** do *not* enter the village but take the middle course between this and the main road and continue ahead along an unsurfaced road lined with trees on the LH side.

This is the road to Bercianos and is used by quite a lot of vehicles, even though it is not (yet) tarred, and produces huge clouds of dust in the dry summer months.

Pass a *laguna* (R) after 1.7km and then, after 2km, the **Ermita de Perales** (L). KSO. After 1km and after crossing the bridge over the **Río Coso** (probably dry) enter the village of…

☎ 5.5km Bercianos del Real Camino (421/357)
Bar, two shops, *hostal*/restaurant, basic *refugio* in old parish house. Church of El Salvador.

Follow the main road through the village. *In the distance you will see the silos of El Burgo Ranero, 7km away. It was in between these two places that the 17th-century Italian pilgrim Domenico Laffi came across the body of a fellow pilgrim who had been devoured by wolves – this has always been one of the loneliest stretches of the entire pilgrimage.*

Continue directly west along the well-defined track, going through the tunnel under the motorway, until you reach the village of…

☎ 8km El Burgo Ranero (429/349)
Shop, bar/restaurant, *hostal*, *refugio*.

Follow the main road through the village past the church (R), cross a road that intersects the village from north to south and pass the cemetery (L).

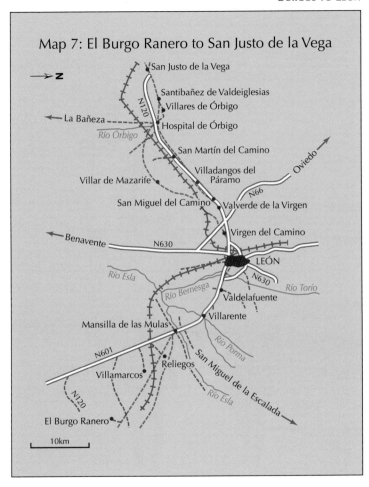

Map 7: El Burgo Ranero to San Justo de la Vega

→ N

San Justo de la Vega

Santibañez de Valdeiglesias

Villares de Órbigo

← La Bañeza

Hospital de Órbigo

Río Órbigo

N120

San Martín del Camino

Villadangos del Páramo

Villar de Mazarife

Oviedo

San Miguel del Camino

Valverde de la Virgen

N66

← Benavente

N630

Virgen del Camino

LEÓN

N630

Río Esla

Río Torío

Río Bernesga

Valdelafuente

Villarente

Mansilla de las Mulas

N601

Río Porma

Reliegos

San Miguel de la Escalada

Villamarcos

N120

Río Esla

El Burgo Ranero

10km

About 4.5km further on on the L is a group of 10 trees *(which you will see before you get to them)* with a brick fountain set back from the road – a good place for a rest. KSO.

The road carries straight on, and after 3.5km more passes a turning, on the L, to the village of **Villamarco** *(the village itself is 1km off route)*.

117

The camino near El Burgo Ranero   (Photo: Paddy Dillon)

About 2km further on the route crosses the railway line and continues with this to its left for a while. The route is still well waymarked with yellow arrows. It enters a small valley, crossing first the 'river' **Valdearcos** and then, 1km further on, the 'river' **Santa María** (usually dried up).

Shortly after this there is another shaded area with trees and the landscape becomes less flat, with *bodegas (storage cellars for keeping wine cool) set into the hilly ground at intervals.* About 2km further on enter...

🏠 13km Reliegos (442/336)

Bar (meals in summer), shop, large *refugio*. Church of SS Cornelio and Cipriano.

KSO through village and out the other side on a stony track across a plain, where you will see *Mansilla de las Mulas* 6km away in the distance. Continue west until you reach the main road (N601), cross it and the bridge over the canal and enter the town.

🏠 6km Mansilla de las Mulas 799m (448/330)

Population 1800. Shops, bars, restaurant, *hostal,* large *refugio*, campsite.
    Town situated on the Río Esla with substantial remains of the 12th-century town walls. 13th-century church of Santa María and Capilla Nuestra Señora de Gracia are all that are left of the town's seven churches, two convents and three pilgrim hospitals.

Continue along the main street to the end of the town and cross the bridge over the **Río Esla**. Fork L onto the old road and then onto a track which continues // to the main road, apart from a few exceptions, for 5km until you reach the village of...

🏠 6km Puente de Villarente (454/324)

Shops, bars, restaurant, *hostal*.
    Small village with a 20-arch curved bridge over the Río Porma.

After the petrol station to the R on leaving Puente de Villarente a path is waymarked to the R which then veers L to run // to but slightly away from the main road on an unsurfaced track. This passes through the small village of **Arcahueja** (4.5km, *bar*) before rejoining the road again at...

6km Valdelafuente (460/318)

Bar/restaurant, *farmacia*, shop in petrol station.

From here you have to continue on the main road, slightly uphill until you reach the **Alto del Portillo**. KSO then, when the bypass (**Avenida de Madrid**) veers R, fork L and continue ahead to cross the **Río Torío** via the **Puente Castro** (FB at side). KSO on **Avenida del Alcalde Miguel Castaño** for 1.5km to the **Plaza Santa Ana**. KSO(R) along the **Calle Barahona, Calle Puertamoneda,** past the church of **Santa María del Mercado** (R), the **Calle de la Rua** and **Calle Ancha** to the cathedral in...

♞ 6.5km León 822m (466.5/311.5)

Population 135,000. All facilities. RENFE. Buses to all major towns. Tourist Office opposite cathedral. Two *refugios*: a) Convento Santa Maria de la Carbajales, Plaza de Santa María 7 (run by the nuns, with volunteer help in summer); b) municipal *refugio*, which shares the same building as the youth hostel, in the Colegio de Huérfanos Ferrovias, Avenida del Parque (near river at entrance to town).

End of the eighth stage in Aymery Picaud's guide and another place worth spending a whole day. The three most important monuments are the 13th-century cathedral in French Gothic style with superb stained-glass windows, the Basilica of San Isidoro containing the Royal Pantheon (with 12th-century wall and ceiling paintings) and a fine Romanesque church of San Marcos, formerly an important pilgrim hospital (now a *parador*). León also contains one of the few Gaudí buildings outside Barcelona: the Casa de las Bottines, once a private house but now a bank.

To leave León: from the cathedral go down the **Calle Sierra Pambrey**, ahead at 'kink' down **Calle Damaso Medina** and turn R into **Calle Cervantes**. Reach the **Plaza Torres de Omaña**, turn L into **Calle Recoleta** and then R into **Calle El Cid**. Reach the **Plaza de San Isidoro** and turn R along walls of San Isidoro (**Avenida de Ramón y Cajal**). Turn L into the **Calle de la Abadía** and continue ahead along **Calle Renueva** and **Avenida de Suero de Quiñones** to the **Plaza San Marcos**.

Cross bridge over **Río Bernesga** by the **Hotel San Marcos**. KSO past public garden (**Parque Quevedo**, *R, good place for rest/picnic; note black swans in lake*) and continue along this road, taking L turning at fork. Cross the railway line by footbridge and KSO, passing the **Iglesia Capilla de Santiago** (R), and KSO, uphill all the time. Turn R at a bus stop and some traffic lights halfway up hill onto the **Camino de la Cruz**, which veers round to the L (still uphill) between *bodegas*. Continue ahead and at junction 300m later with another track coming from L KSO(L) on unsurfaced road by scrap dealers.

This may sound complicated, but all you are doing is playing 'hide and seek' to avoid the main road.

KSO ahead, passing factories, forking R uphill (away from main road) at marble factory. At top of hill continue on track coming from L *(the very tall spire of the modern church of Virgen del Camino is visible ahead)* and take next L fork by long wall on R.

At start of residential area (**Calle Tras las Casas**) *fork* (not turn) L onto tarred road ahead *(leading towards church spire)*. Continue down **Calle del Orbigo** and take second L into the **Calle Cervantes** and then turn R onto main road, continuing to church in...

♟ 7.5km Virgen del Camino 905m (474/304)

Large village (now a suburb of León) with shops, bars, restaurant, *hostal*.

Church of San Froilan (modern) has a very interesting façade which includes 13 huge bronze statues, one of which is St James pointing the way to Santiago. Its interior is very plain apart from an extremely ornate baroque reredos, retained from a former church on this site.

Cross the road after (visiting) the church and continue on minor road downhill behind crash barrier (to L) (signposted 'Fresno del Camino 3.5km') and leading to cemetery.

About 100m later the two caminos *divide. From here to Hospital de Orbigo (some 25km, according to which route you choose) you have two options: a) the traditional historic (road) route via Villadangos del Páramo (22km) and b) a longer but very much quieter alternative which passes to the south of the N120 on minor roads via Villar de Mazarife (31km) (see page 123 below). Both are waymarked.*

A: ROAD OPTION VIA VILLADANGOS DEL PARAMO
In the next section you basically follow the road but often take parallel tracks to avoid actually walking along it.

Continue up hill past cemetery (L) and rejoin road in front of a factory. Continue on path above road (L): ahead you can see a (complicated) motorway junction.

When you rejoin the road cross the first part (a sliproad) carefully, crossing where you see the yellow arrows painted on the road itself, and walk on the hard shoulder of the main Madrid–Astorga road. KSO, go under *both* bridges and KSO. Continue along the road.

3km Valverde de la Virgen 887m (477/301)
Bar, *fuente*.

1km San Miguel del Camino (478/300)

Shortly after San Miguel fork L off road onto track // to it. Veer R at farm and follow track across open land more or less // to road. When you think you are going to rejoin the road KSO instead down dip to track // to road. KSO.

♙ 5.5km Urbanización de Santiago (483.5/294.5)
Two *hostales*.

Continue on road to…

♙ 1.5km Villadangos del Páramo (485/293)
Shops, bars, *hostal*, pharmacy, restaurant. *Refugio* in old school on main road at entrance to village.

Originally a Roman town. Church of Santiago has a painting of Santiago Matamoros on main west portal and statues of the saint both as 'moor slayer' and as 'pilgrim' at side of main altarpiece. (The word 'páramo' in this and many other place names means 'bleak plateau'.)

Cross road at entrance to village (refugio *on R*), fork R and enter village. Turn L at end to return to main road for a short while. Then fork L off it onto a track // to road. Follow this for as far as is practicable and then rejoin road to walk on hard shoulder.

Unfortunately there is no alternative to the road in this section as all the land to L and R of the road is criss-crossed with canals, dykes and deep irrigation channels.

Continue to…

4km San Martín del Camino (489/299)
Small shop, two bars.

KSO and shortly outside village cross road and fork R onto track // to road. At farm veer slightly R to pass it (on your L) then veer L again to follow track // to road. KSO until, after 2km, the track forks away from the road. Turn L, cross bridge over dyke and return to road over crash barrier.

KSO. About 1.5km before **Hospital de Orbigo,** opposite a gravel works, turn R down a lane. Follow path through fields to town, veering L at fork into the **Calle Orbigo** along the river and then turn L to cross the bridge over the river into…

7km Hospital de Orbigo 819m (496/282)

Continue as described on page 125.

B: COUNTRY ROUTE VIA VILLAR DE MAZARIFE
This is sometimes sparsely waymarked but is easy enough to follow.

Turn L off main road and veer L up side of wall uphill. KSO ahead. Join minor road coming from back R and KSO along it. Ignore next L turn, KSO downhill and go *under* road to enter…

2km Fresno del Camino
Fountain.

KSO ahead uphill *(unmarked bar in social club on R)* on road marked 'Oncina de la Valdoncina'. Go downhill, crosss minor railway line, bridge over stream *(probably dry, small fountain/water supply to L)* and enter village of…

2km Oncina del la Valdoncina

Veer R then L uphill and KSO on stony track (sign to 'Chozas de Abajo, 5km'). Continue uphill to open plateau, fork and then veer L. Continue ahead on open plateauland, more or less flat, ignoring turns to L and R. Cross minor road and enter…

5.5km Chozas de Abajo
Bar (meals), camping.

KSO(R) on **Calle Real** (signed 'Villar de Mazarife, 4km'). Turn L and then R in village, cross bridge and KSO on unsurfaced road, ignoring turns, to…

4.5km Villar de Mazarife
Two bars, shop, *mesón*, spartan *refugio*.

Continue to **Plaza Mediovilla** and ahead along **Calle Camino** to road (**Carretera Valcabo**). Cross it and KSO (signposted 'Villavente 9.3km') on minor tarred road, past sports ground (L). KSO.

The páramo is almost completely flat (if, in fact, the earth is…), with cornfields, sunflowers in season, irrigation channels and the occasional tree. The Montes de León are visible away to your R on the horizon (and, later, gradually ahead of you). Few waymarks in this area as there is little else to do but continue straight ahead.

After 6km cross a minor road and continue ahead on what has now become an unsurfaced road, turning L at small junction of similar tracks 100m later. Cross bridge over canal, veer R and KSO, ignoring turns to L or R. After 2km cross bridge over a large canal and then a road and KSO again into…

10km Villavante
Two bars (no food), shop.

Turn R into village at junction with tarred road and then L into **Calle Santa María**.
124

Crossing the bleak páramo *on the way from León to Hospital de Órbigo* (Photo: Paddy Dillon)

Turn R *after* junction with the **Calle Pradico** and veer L into another street. Turn L again at bar down **Calle Iglesia**.

Pass church (on your R) and KSO, forking L down side of huge water tower. Cross bridge over railway line *(a notice at start says 'Hospital de Orbigo, 3.5km')*.

Turn L along minor road at end of bridge, continue on unsurfaced road after last house, along side of railway track (it is on your L) at first, then veering R towards **Hospital de Orbigo** *(visible ahead)*.

KSO for 2km, cross minor road, continue ahead (still on unsurfaced road). About 600m later reach minor road *(fountain on R)*, passing between factory buildings. Turn R, cross main road (N120) carefully and continue ahead on **Avenida de la Constitución** into **Hospital de Orbigo** (4km).

🏠 7km Hospital de Orbigo 819m (496/282)

Small town, population 1320, with shops, *hostal*, restaurant, campsite, two fountains. Two *refugios* a) in parish house, at no 32 on main street b) municipal *refugio* in wooded grounds of campsite.

The longest pilgrim bridge in Spain, crossing the river Orbigo. It is 204m long and has 20 arches. It is known as the bridge of the Paso Honroso in memory of a month-long jousting tournament which took place in 1434, breaking 300 lances and leaving one person dead. Its champions continued to Santiago where they left a golden necklace on the processional statue of Santiago Menor (reportedly still there).

Bodegas, after Hospital de Orbigo
(Photo: Ysabel Halpin)

Cross Roman bridge and continue ahead, passing **Casa Consistorial** (R, *fountain opposite on L*), church of **Santa María** (R), and KSO down main street to end of town (down the **Calle Camino de Santiago**). At the crossroads with an unsurfaced road at the end you again have two options:

a) KSO *(waymarked)* to continue on the road (the historic route) to Astorga, or

b) *(also waymarked)* turn R for an alternative country route as far as San Justo de la Vega where both options meet up (the one described here).

KSO along minor road to...

2km Villares de Orbigo 919m (498/280)
Small shop, bar.

Ignore turns to L and R. Enter village, turn L then R, then veer R (past *lavadero*). Veer L and then turn R onto road, cross it (and canal) and KSO. After 200m turn L up junction with green lane, KSO for 1km and join road again. Turn R to village of...

⚫ 2.5km Santibañez de Valdeiglesias 845m (500.5/277.5)
Bar (no food), refugio.

Enter village down **Camino Villares** and continue ahead down **Calle Real** then turn R up **Calle Carromonte Alto** and KSO, uphill all the time, into open country.

At top of hill descend to take L fork, past large sandstone quarry to L. Descend to wide shallow valley *(watch out for waymarks on the ground)* and then KSO ahead up other side, taking RH fork part way up. KSO then take L at next fork, uphill all the time.

At top of hill join track coming from back L and KSO downhill ahead. Take RH fork (four options to L) and go uphill under trees to open plateau. *(HT cables ahead, woods to L ahead.)* Descend to next valley (line of trees along stream) and then up again to another open plateau.

At junction of similar tracks when you are level with *second* farm building to R veer L under electric cables *(view of Astorga ahead, below)*, taking RH of two forks leading to the **Crucero de Santo Toribio**.

Splendid views of Astorga. Toribio, along with Genadio (both from Astorga), Isidore of Seville and Ildefonso of Toledo, were the four bishop saints. This is where this camino *joins the other one coming from Hospital de Orbigo along the road.*

Go downhill ahead and 200m later turn R onto section of old main road which then leads to the new one. Continue along it into…

🚏 8km San Justo de la Vega (508.5/269.5)

Bars, restaurants, shop, *hostal*, camping by river in summer.
    Church with old tower but very modern windows and brick nave.

Continue through village and out along main road until you have crossed the road bridge over the **Río Tuerto**. Turn R 100m after bend onto unsurfaced road marked *'merendero'* (picnic area) then L along a shaded lane // to the road. Follow this for 2km past field, factory and another field until you cross an old three-arched bridge over a small canal. Turn L onto unsurfaced road and KSO to main road. Turn R along it, cross two level crossings. Turn R along this road, cross two level crossings and follow road uphill into town. Turn R to visit cathedral.

🚏 3.5km Astorga 869m (512/266)

Population 14,000, all facilities. RENFE. Buses to Madrid, León, Ponferrada and Villafranca del Bierzo. Tourist Office opposite cathedral. Large *refugio* in centre (160pl).

    A town dating from Roman times, with extensive remains of its original town walls behind the cathedral. Astorga was (and still is) the junction of two major pilgrim routes: the *Camino francés* (described here) and the *Camino mozárabe* or *Vía de la Plata*. This explains the unusually large number of pilgrim hospitals formerly in existence (there were 22 in the Middle Ages), the last of which, the Hospital de las Cinco Llagas ('the Five Wounds'), burned down early in the 20th century. Gothic cathedral with interesting choir stalls and museum. Bishop's Palace built by the Catalan architect Antonio Gaudí, with pilgrim museum. Several other interesting churches, Baroque town hall. It is worth spending half a day here.

Between Astorga and Ponferrada the camino passes through the isolated area of the Maragatería (as far as the Cruz de Ferro) and then into the Bierzo region, which continues until you leave the province of León and enter Galicia. For many people this is one of the most beautiful stretches of the camino, most of it in the Montes de León, but as there are few villages, bars or shops along the way it is advisable to carry a certain amount of food and water. Since the route is also quite high (the Cruz de Ferro is at 1504m) warm clothing is needed, even in summer.

Much of the camino between Astorga and Molinaseca is on the road or on pilgrim andaderos (specially prepared pistes to the side) but it is very quiet and there is very little traffic.

To leave Astorga: turn L at traffic lights on main road out of Astorga to the west onto minor road signposted 'Santa Colomba de Somoza' and 'Castrillo de

Astorga, Bishop's palace

los Polvazares'. KSO to **Valdeviejas**, passing a memorial sign (L) to 'peregrinos identes' and then an old people's complex (L). Pass the **Ermita Ecco Homo** (L) and then KSO on road.

Cross the motorway and continue on *piste* on RH side of road. Rejoin road to cross bridge over the river **Río Jerga** and 200m later, at entrance board to Murias, fork L off road onto a track leading into…

Map 8: San Justo de la Vega to Villafranca del Bierzo

♣ 5km Murias de Rechivaldo 882m (517/261)

Bar (no shop), *mesón, refugio* at end of village on road.

Church of San Esteban (18th century), the first of the many churches you will see in the Maragatería with an *espadaña*, a bell tower with an (often lengthy) outside stone staircase to reach it.

Pass along the side of the village to its L. Enter street (**Camino de Santiago**) and continue along it to the end *(turn R for refugio)*, when it becomes a track leading to open country.

About 1km further on a short detour is recommended to **Castrillo de los Polvazares**, *a cobbled village typical of the Maragatería, in a very fine state of preservation and a National Monument. Bars, restaurants (all offer* cocido maragato *but as this is* extremely filling make sure you do not have to walk very far after lunch...). To leave you can either retrace your steps or continue on a FP, leading straight ahead all the time, directly to Santa Catalina de Somoza.*

KSO on *piste* for 2km, until you reach the road. Cross over and KSO ahead (signposted 'El Ganso 5') and KSO to village of...

♣ 5km Santa Catalina de Somoza 977m (522/256)

Two bars, *refugio*.

Fork R at entrance to village along lane towards church and KSO along **Calle Real**. Rejoin road at large wooden wayside cross with seats and KSO along road for a short distance then *piste* starts again. Continue to...

Modern St James outside bar in El Ganso
(Photo: Ysabel Halpin)

♣ 4km El Ganso 1020m (526/252)

Two bars in summer, very basic *refugio*.

Small village which formerly had a monastery and pilgrim hospital. Church of Santiago, with chapel of Cristo de los Peregrinos.

Fork R at entrance to village along lane (village to your L). KSO and then turn L back onto road at church. KSO along road, passing a turning to Rabanal Viejo after 3km, at the **Puente Pañote**: do *not* take this but KSO ahead to…

🏠 7km Rabanal del Camino 1149m (533/245)

Two *hostal*-restaurants, three *refugios* (two all year), shop in summer, fountain.

End of the ninth stage in Aymery Picaud's guide. Ermita del Santo Cristo at entrance to village, church of San José and parish church of Santa María. Today the population is only 27, except in summer when migrants return for their holidays, but in former times it was an important pilgrim halt and much larger (as the presence of three churches testifies).

The village has come back to life in the last few years, however, due to the pilgrim route and its Benedictine monastery, the Monasterio de San Salvador del Monte Irago. This was founded by four monks, originally from Santo Domingo de Silos (near Burgos), but is now affiliated to the large Benedictine missionary abbey of St Otilien (near Munich). Their mission is to attend to the (spiritual) needs of pilgrims. They sing Laudes every morning in the parish church, Vespers and Compline every evening (all three in Gregorian chant), plus a daily morning mass, and the church of Santa María is now open all day.

Turn R off road after cemetery church (L) to enter village. Pass churches of **San José** and **Santa María** and the two *hostales* and KSO along green lane for 1km to rejoin road again. KSO ahead along it. *(Fountain to R of road after 2km at KM 25, with icy cold water.)* Continue to climb and KSO up to…

6km Foncebadón 1495m (539/239)

Bar/*méson* in summer. *Refugio* built in former church of Santa María not yet open due to problems with water supply. Hotel/restaurant under construction.

This village, too, is very slowly beginning to come back to life. It was almost abandoned until recently (there were only two inhabitants left, plus a few more in summer), though in the 12th century the hermit Gaucelmo built a church, hospital and hospice for pilgrims, of which the remains still exist (as you leave the village). There was a considerable population in the past, as is evident from the numerous ruined houses.

Fork L off road, enter village and continue to end. KSO, passing ruined church and rejoin road after 1km. Turn L and 300m further on reach the…

Camino at entry to Foncebadón
(Photo: Ysabel Halpin)

2km Cruz de Ferro 1504m (541/237)

A very tall iron cross atop a huge cairn. Traditionally pilgrims brought a stone with them from home to add to the pile. Fantastic views on a clear day, with Monte Teleno (the highest mountain in the whole area, 2188m) in the distance to the south. Modern Ermita de Santiago, built in the 1982 Holy Year. From here the route is almost all downhill to Ponferrada, some 25km away.

[RJ]: turn R off road between 21st and 22nd snow pole on road after passing the cross. If you miss it, continue along the road to rejoin the *camino* at the entrance to Foncebadón].

KSO on road, passing highest point of the entire route (at 1517m) to another almost abandoned village of…

2km Manjarín 1451m (543/235)

Another small, almost abandoned village *(fountain on L on leaving)*. Small, extremely spartan *refugio*. Former church was dedicated to San Roque.

Continue on road for 2km, pass turning to military base *(visible on hill above road, with radar, etc)* and KSO. *Mountain ranges visible ahead of you and to the L.*

After 1–2km watch out for a turning off the road to the R 200m after road KM 37 and 100m after an iron cross on R. Fork R off road on path which climbs up

132

Cruz de Ferro

between two small hills; this short-cuts some of the many hairpins and cuts off quite a long section of the road, which you rejoin on the other side *(good view of Ponferrada ahead)*. [RJ: turn L uphill, near drain, before road veers R.]

About 400m further on fork L off road onto FP going downhill below the road (which remains on your R). Continue along it, descending steeply, until, abruptly, you reach the slate-roofed village of…

🕮 7km El Acebo 1156m (550/228)

Fountain on roadside as you leave the FP and two others in village. Two bar/restaurants (no shop), two *refugios* (one municipal, one private).

Another village which formerly had a pilgrim hospital. A single long, narrow street whose old houses have overhanging balconies at first-floor level and outside staircases, their slate roofs a sudden change from the red pantiles encountered up to now. Church has statue of Santiago Peregrino.

KSO through village, past *ermita* and cemetery and a *memorial in the form of an iron bicycle sculpture to a German pilgrim killed there whilst cycling to Santiago in 1987.* KSO on the road to continue *and if you do not want to make the detour described here turn to page 135.*

OPTIONAL DETOUR VIA THE VALLE DEL SILENCIO

In good weather fit pilgrims interested in Mozárabic churches can make a detour on foot from here to **Peñalba de Santiago** *(23km), set in the Valle del Silencio, and then continue directly from there to Ponferrada (30km) by a very minor road, visiting the former monastery of* **San Pedro de Montes de Valdueza** *en route as well. It is not waymarked but is easy enough to follow. (Take food and water with you.)*

To do so turn L at the end of the village in **El Acebo**, after the *ermita* and the bicycle memorial, down a minor tarred road marked 'Compludo'. Continue downhill all the time to the valley botom, turn R at the junction to *Carascedo de Compludo*, then pass the *Herrerías (forge of Roman origin)*. Continue through the village of **Compludo** (4km, *small bar*), passing the church of **Santos Justo y Pastor** *(all that is left of the large monastery village founded by San Fructuoso in the 7th century)* and then veer R uphill up a clear, unsurfaced road. This leads along the mountainside, undulating, until you reach the road (church to R) at entrance to the village of **Espinoso de Compudo** (5km).

Turn L along the road to bend then *fork* L off it onto a track. This is not always very clear but before you start you can see your next objective – the village of *San Cristobo* – ahead on a ridge in front of you. The track takes you down and up out of two valleys en route.

When you reach **San Cristobo** (5km) turn L along road through village *(bar/restaurant on L)* and at the end turn R along a very clear, newly prepared unsurfaced road (presumably waiting to be tarmacked once the landslide has been cleared) which takes you more or less on the level, winding its way along the side of the mountains, all the way to

Peñalba de Santiago (7km)

The village of Peñalba de Santiago (ask in 'cantina' – bar with meals – about rooms) takes its name from the 'white rock' (*alba, peña*) on the other side of the valley and grew up around the monastery founded by San Genadio (a former bishop of Astorg) in the10th century. It was dedicated to St James but the church is all that remains today. There were numerous monasteries, religious communities and isolated anchorites living in caves in this part of the Bierzo during the Visigothic period, and it is thought that there were as many as 2000 monks in this cave-ridden area at that time The present church, built by Salomón (a disciple of San Gebadio) between AD931 and 937, is in good condition and now serves as the parish church. It is open to visitors (closed Sunday evenings and all day Mondays) and is well worth a visit.

A FP leads from the village (start near bar) to the **Cueva de San Genadio** *(cave chapel), one hour on foot in each direction.*

Continue to *Ponferrada* on the road, turning L (signposted) to make a detour to the village of **San Pedro de Montes** and its former monastery. *The church is still intact and is open to visitors (same hours as Peñalba de Santiago), as are the ruins of the monastery buildings (apparently there are plans to restore these as a guest-house/retreat/study centre some time in the future).*

To continue you do not need to return to the road immediately but can follow a track which leaves the village past the small ermita which you will see on the hillside over to your R as you enter. This leads down to the road eventually, before the village of **San Clemente.** *Continue from there via* **San Esteban, San Lorenzo** *and* **Otero,** *entering Ponferrada from the south, where you will rejoin the main camino just before you cross the bridge over the* **Río Boeza.**

Continue as described on page 137 below.

To continue without making the detour: KSO ahead out of *El Acebo* on the road. About 1km before the next village of *Riego de Ambrós*, visible ahead, watch out for a turning to L off road just before a bend onto a FP below the road. Follow this down to the village.

In the section from Foncebadón to Riego de Ambrós there are a lot of wayside crosses with scallop shells below: memorials to pilgrims who died en route?

☎ 3.5km Riego de Ambrós 920m (553.5/224.5)

Two bars, shop, fountain, *refugio* by church, *mesón* on main road (rooms).

Enter village, follow street straight on (downhill all the time) and then turn R down a grassy lane. Continue downhill through trees for 1km (in a straight line all the time), then join a farm track. Join a road a few metres further on and turn L along it. About 80m after this turn R off the road to a track. KSO then fork R downhill and zigzag down to clearing in a wood with enormous chestnut trees. KSO downhill.

After a while, although the path remains level, the land falls away into a valley so that you are actually walking quite high up here, in an area perfumed with cistus (a bush that smells like church incense).

Track veers R and eventually descends to the road. About 100m before this turn L along track coming from R. After this you can either turn L to road (at bridge) or continue for a short while longer up hill to R on path, joining road further down at a large wayside cross. After that continue down the road to large village of...

🏛 **4.5km Molinaseca 595m (558/220)**

Shops, bars, restaurants, *hostal*, two *fondas. Refugio* at end of village in former church (Ermita de San Roque). Swimming area in river by bridge (water is icy, even in summer).

Enter village passing **Ermita de las Angustias** (R), partly set into the cliffs, and cross the Romanesque **Puente de los Peregrinos** over the **Río Meruelo**. Continue along the **Calle Real** (the main street) and when this runs into the main road KSO along it until you reach a tennis court on your R. Turn off road to R and then turn L along a lane // to road. KSO along it as it passes behind the houses on the main road, cross a minor road and KSO slightly uphill along the side of fields. Rejoin road at the top of the hill, just before a crossroads. At top of hill road goes downhill.

Good view of Ponferrada ahead (church tower to LH side is the Basilica de la Encina). About 100m later you have a choice of two routes into Ponferrada, both waymarked), R or L. The RH route is slightly shorter, much of it on a busy road; the LH route is slightly longer and is not particularly scenic but it does take you onto quieter roads with a great deal less traffic and some parts also have more shade.

🏛 **LH ROUTE VIA CAMPO**

Fork L down minor road and then KSO(L) after 50m down earth track. Fork L again 100m later downhill on earth/grassy track/lane, which climbs uphill again after going over a stream. KSO (uphill) at crossing with similar track (vines to your L). [RJ: KSO at R fork uphill.]

KSO downhill again. About 1.5km after making your LH/RH choice enter village of **Campo** (3km).

Take RH fork down **Calle Real** *(lined with old houses on both sides. Stone sitting area at junction).* [RJ: fork R at two earth tracks at top of *Calle Real*.] *(18th-century church to L.)*

At small plaza at the bottom of the **Calle Real** continue ahead along LH of two roads (no name at start) which is gravelled and, later, tarred. KSO(L) at junction with **Calle de los Mesones** passing through waste ground, sports ground (to R), past rubbish tip, slaughterhouse and large factory. KSO at 'stop' sign. [RJ: L fork at junction.] About 500m further on road runs into a (more) main road coming from back L. *Bar at crossing.* [RJ: take LH fork marked 'Los Barrios'.]

Continue 100m to next junction *(shop to the L)* and turn R to cross the medieval **Puente Mascarón** over the **Río Boeza** to enter *Ponferrada*. Then:

a) *if you are continuing* turn L on other side up **Calle Camino Bajo de San Andres**, go under railway line and uphill. At the junction at the top KSO(L) along **Calle Buenavista** and then R almost immediately along **Calle Hospital**

(15th-century Hospital de la Reina at no 28). Turn L at top then R up **Calle Gil y Carrasco** *(up side of castle, Tourist Office on L)* and follow it uphill into the **Plaza Virgen de la Encina**.

b) *if you want to sleep in the* refugio KSO ahead after crossing bridge, use pavement to RH side of road and shortly before you reach a roundabout turn R across waste ground to the *refugio*, a large purpose-built modern construction next to the former cemetery church *(Iglesia del Carmen)*.

RH (ROAD) ROUTE

KSO ahead on road for 1.5km and veer R at fork by furniture warehouse, just before KM 54. Continue downhill, cross bridge over **Río Boeza** and shortly afterwards take path beside road on LH side. Veer slightly L off road behind factory 500m later and KSO along lane between low walls with fields on either side, following HT lines. After 1km fork R uphill, cross bridge over railway line, veer L along cemetery wall to *refugio*.

Continue ahead to join **Avenida del Castillo**, turn R at roundabout with modern *crucero* (**Calle Cruz de Miranda**) and then immediately L (**Calle del Pregonero**). KSO, continue on **Avenida del Castillo** and then turn R up pedestrianised street (**Calle Gil y Carrasco**) between *castillo* and church of **San Andrés**. Continue uphill to the **Plaza de la Encina** and the basilica.

🏛 8km Ponferrada 543m (566/212)

Population 50,000. All facilities, RENFE, large *refugio* at entrance to town. Tourist Office.

Large industrial town in two parts at the junction of the rivers Boeza and Sil, taking its name from the iron bridge over the latter. (Today a metal bridge is nothing surprising but it was a luxury when it was built, at the end of the 12th century, and only possible in an area rich in iron.) The new part of the town is on the west side of the river Sil, the small historic part on the east, with the 13th-century castle built by the Knights Templar, the 16th-century basilica of Nuestra Señora de la Encina (Our Lady of the Evergreen Oak), 17th-century town hall and 16th-century Torre del Reloj, the only surviving remnant of the former town walls. The 10th-century mozarabic church of Santo Tomás de Ollas is in the suburbs, to the north of the town (and where the *camino* originally passed).

To continue (the exit from Ponferrada is both ugly and tedious): from the **Plaza de la Encina** next to the **basilica** veer L across square, go down flight of steps and KSO down **Calle Rañadero** *(stepped street)*. Turn L at bottom *(post office* *to R)* and cross **Río Sil (Avenida de Puebla)**. About 200m later turn R down **Calle Río Urdiales** which veers L into a big square/parking lot. KSO and at junction turn R down wide tree-lined avenue **(Avenida del Sacramento)**. KSO at roundabout *(with fountain and sculptures)*. KSO, veering L uphill to junction with another tree-lined avenue and turn R **(Avenida de la Libertad)** passing large slag heaps on your L.

Turn L (signposted 'Compostilla,' *sic*) along road and at end (by Red Cross post) turn R and then immediately L to KSO under flats and then emerge in **Plaza de Compostilla** *(garden with seats)*.

Continue ahead, passing to L of church of **Santa María de Compostilla** *(note modern statue to L, opposite entrance, and modern murals, painted in the 1993 Holy Year, in entrance arcade)*. Cross road, continue down **IV Avenida** *(note private house on your L with two very tall chimneys, one of which has a stork's nest on top)* and through a residential area *(with numbered, not named, streets)*. Turn L then R (into **3a Traversia**) past tennis courts (on L) and the **Ermita** (not church) of **Nuestra Señora de Compostilla** *(modern mural at end)* and modern *cruceiro (St James the pilgrim is on one side, the Virgin and Child on the other)*.

KSO ahead then continue on FP then minor road (in a straight line all the time). Pass under motorway and fork L then KSO(L) to church of…

5km Columbrianos (571/207)

Church has a large covered porch on other side, with seats – a good place for a rest, plus view of the mountains.

KSO ahead downhill **(Calle El Teso)** and KSO(R) to cross busy road via pedestrian crossing. KSO ahead down **Calle la Iglesia** then fork R into the **Calle Real**.

Turn L by small church **(Capilla de San Blas,** *bar to R)* and continue down **Calle San Blas** (not marked at start) with fields to either side. Cross minor railway line and KSO for 2km, ignoring turns to L or R. Road joins from back L [RJ: L fork – earth road], which becomes **Calle Paraiso** in…

2.5km Fuentesnuevas (573.5/204.5)

Bar.

Emerge at crossing, continue on **Calle Real** *(bar on R, cruceiro to L)* in village and KSO, passing church (on your R) and then continue through fields for 1.5km until track joins road (from back L) in…

2km Camponaraya 490m (575.5/202.5)

A very long, straggling village with shops, bars, bank.

Turn R onto road [RJ: turn L at house no 337] and continue through village past church and over **Río Naraya.**

At the end (1km), when the NVI veers R (wine cooperative to your L) KSO(L) uphill *(fountain and seats on L)* on earth road/track through vines.

From here you can see the mountains of the El Bierzo region all round you and the camino *leads through orchards and vines for much of the time.*

Cross bridge over motorway, turn L on other side and KSO(R) through vines for 1.5km. Cross a road and KSO on other side on the *camino* (now tarmacked) to...

⊞ 5.5km Cacabelos 483m (581/197)

Shops, bars, restaurant, *hostal*, bank. Large municipal *refugio* next to church after crossing Río Cua. Swimming area in the river. One of the last storks on the *camino* has its 'residence' on the church of the Sanctuario de las Angustias on leaving the town (though others have been reported near the Castillo in Villafranca del Bierzo).

Cacabelos was formerly an important pilgrim town, with five hospitals, including San Lázaro, built in 1237 on the site of the present Moncloa restaurant (on your L at entrance). On leaving the town note old wine press to RH side of road.

Go downhill into the town, KSO down main street, pass 15th-century **Capilla de San Roque** (R) and continue down pedestrianised street. (*If you turn L you emerge into a tree-lined square with seats, shade, shops.*) Pass to L of church and KSO down **Calle de las Angustias.** Continue ahead, cross bridge over river *(swimming area in summer when it is dammed up)* and KSO on main road (refugio *on L adjoining Santuario de la Virgen de las Angustias*).

Continue on road for 2km past hamlet of **Pierros** *(fountain by bus shelter and two other unmarked ones)*. Continue on road to road KM 406 then turn R up earth track that veers L uphill, diagonally R away from the road. Continue on this track until you reach the Romanesque **Iglesia de Santiago** (L), by cemetery on the outskirts of **Villafranca del Bierzo**.

♟ 7km Villafranca del Bierzo 511m (588/190)

Small town with all facilities, several *hostales*. Two *refugios*, plus tented *base de acampada* in summer. Tourist Office in Calle Alameda Alta, near church of San Nicolás.

The Iglesia de Santiago has a finely carved Puerta del Perdón on its north side, through which pilgrims who were too weak, ill or injured to continue to Santiago entered in order to obtain the same indulgences and remission of their sins as they would have done had they completed their pilgrimage. Two *refugios* near church: municipal one on R (closed in winter), the other, on L, the 'Ave Fenix', is on the site of a medieval hospice and is run by an association (open all year but still being renovated, to replace an earlier one destroyed by fire, hence its name).

The end of the tenth stage in Aymery Picaud's guide. There are a number of other interesting churches including 16th-century Colegiata de Santa María, 17th-century Anunciada and 17th-century convent church of San Francisco with Baroque cloister. The Castillo-Palacio de los Marqueses (now privately owned) dates from the 15th century and the Calle del Agua contains some fine 18th-century houses, many with armorial devices above the doors.

Between Villafranca and the small Galician village of O Cebreiro at 1300m and 30km away there are more mountains and a very stiff climb, whether you opt for one of the two high-level routes or the lower one along the old (and some parts of the new) main road. If you intend to spend the night in O Cebreiro make sure you leave Villafranca early in the day.

From the **Iglesia de Santiago** go downhill to the **Castillo** and take second turn R downhill at side of castle (**Calle Salinas**). Cross street, go down stone staircase then a flight of steps and KSO past a small square and the *Correos* along the **Calle del Agua.** Turn sharp L at the bottom **(Plazuela Santa Catalina)** into the **Cuesta de Zamora** and cross the bridge over the **Río Burbia** *(modern statue of St James at start of bridge).*

After this you have three choices (all waymarked): a low-level route along the road in the valley (playing 'hide and seek' with the motorway bridges and using sections of the old main road where the new one has been straightened out); a (slightly longer) higher-level route to the R of the main road, passing near Pradela, both of which join up in Trabadelo either 10 or 12km later; and a longer, strenuous option, very beautiful in good weather, which passes high up to the left of the main road via Dragonte, Moral de Valcarce, Vilar de Corrales, San Fiz de Seo and Villasinde, rejoining the other two routes in Herrerías, 8km before O Cebreiro.

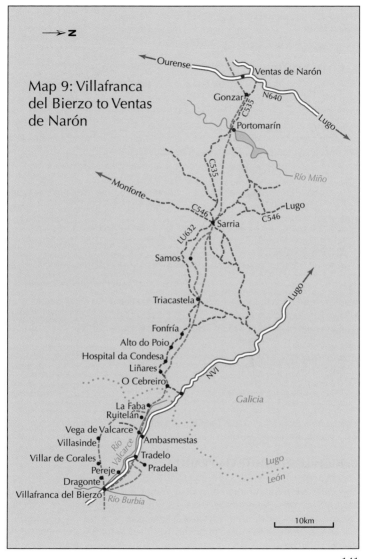

Map 9: Villafranca del Bierzo to Ventas de Narón

The route you take will be determined by how fit you are (don't take the high-level options if you have bad knees) and the weather: neither high-level option is recommended if it is foggy or raining heavily.

A: ROAD ROUTE

Take this option in bad weather. Flat but very busy, with a lot of heavy traffic. Normally you should walk on the LH side, facing the oncoming vehicles, but you may decide it is wiser, when there are LH bends, to cross over to the other side temporarily so that you can be seen more easily.

After crossing the **Río Burbia** continue ahead, passing convent and **Iglesia de la Concepción** (on L) and KSO. After 1km you reach the exit of the road tunnel under the mountains on leaving the town (L) and the new *autopista* on 'legs' in front of you. Cross over *very* carefully and turn R.

KSO for 3km (sometimes it is possible to walk on the inside of the crash barrier). At KM 410 turn R onto a section of the *old* NVI and 500m later enter village of...

🏠 5km Pereje

Bar, *refugio* at end of village on L.

KSO(R) ahead on main street (**Calle Camino de Santiago**) and continue to end of village. Return to main road for 2.5km (*Río Valcarce* still to your L). Fork L onto section of old road at KM 413 and continue for 1km to...

🏠 3.5km Trabadelo

Hostal/resaurant and *mesón* both on main road near middle of village, *panadería* on main street at end.

Continue on main street (**Calle Camino de Santiago**), pass church (*fountain*) and KSO as described on page 143.

B: HIGH-LEVEL ROUTE VIA PRADELA

This high-level route is also waymarked and is much quieter, with superb views on a clear day. It is much more strenuous, climbs very steeply to start with and descends very steeply to Trabadelo, but is worth it unless the weather is bad. The NVI is visible most of the time way below in the valley to the L.

To take this option cross the bridge over the **Río Burbia** and then fork R steeply uphill between houses (**Calle Pradra**). This continues to climb steadily for nearly 3km, after which the track levels out somewhat, climbing more gradually and following the shoulder of the hillside. *Splendid views on a clear day.*

KSO, ignoring RH turns and KSO(R) at fork on higher path, to pass to RH side of grove of trees on skyline ahead.

After passing below TV masts (up to R) the *camino* starts to descend gradually. Shortly afterwards the village of *Pradela* becomes visible ahead when you reach a junction. Turn L *(RH turn goes to Pradela – fountain but no other facilities)*. At next junction KSO(L) ahead through chestnut woods for 500m, in a straight line except for a 'kink' halfway to the road.

When you reach the road cross over and go down gravel path to RH side of road, descending steeply all the time, zigzagging down to reach road at electric pylons.

Follow road for 60m then fork R down another steep gravel track, zigzagging all the time. Cross road again and continue ahead down shady walled lane, which brings you out in the village of **Trabadelo**. Turn L down concrete lane to church *(fountain)* and turn R along main street to continue.

⌂ 12km Trabadelo (600/178)

Continue on main street (**Calle Camino de Santiago**), rising gently all the time *(panadería on R near end of village)*.

At junction with turn to *Pradela* KSO(L) ahead on old road till you come to where the motorway crosses the NVI. Turn R along main road (changing sides as necessary), crossing and recrossing the **Río Valcarce** several times. Continue on NVI until just after the **Hostal Valcarce** at road KM 418 *(bar/restaurant, rooms, shop, CD)*.

About 200m later fork L on the old road into **Portela** *(fountain, bar/mesón)*. Rejoin NVI at end of hamlet, turning L to continue on main road again. About 500m later, at junction, KSO(L) marked 'Ambasmestas' and 'Vega de Valcarce' (turn onto *old* road alongside **Río Valcarce,** to your L). Continue ahead to small village of...

4.5km Ambasmestas (604.5/173/5)

Two bars (one with restaurant), *panadería*, fountain.

Continue ahead on road through **Ambascasas** (you now have the viaduct high above you to the R) and KSO to...

🏠 2.5m Vega de Valcarce 630m (607/171)

Shops, bars, *farmacía*, bank, *fonda, refugio* in centre of village.

The **Castillo de Sarracin** is visible above the village to the L. To visit it – for the view, as it is in ruins – ask if you can leave your rucksack in one of the bars and go up on foot, 20min each way. Go up road marked 'Barjas' and then fork R onto a track leading straight up to it.

After Vega de Valcarce the camino starts to climb, gently at first and then steeply, up to O Cebreiro. To begin with it continues to follow the course of the Río Valcarce but then wends its way up through chestnut woods, tiny villages and then open country where it enters Galicia at 1200m.

Continue on the road to…

🏠 2km Ruitelán (609/169)

Two bars (one with shop), *refugio*. Chapel of San Froilán.

Just before road bends round uphill to R, fork L downhill into…

🏠 1km Herrerías 680m (610/168)

Veer R over the river *(the Dragonte* variante *rejoins the* Camino francés *here from the L)* and then turn to page 147 to continue.

C: HIGH-LEVEL ROUTE VIA DRAGONTE

This is a considerably longer option but worth it in good weather (providing you have already come a long way and are therefore fit). Strenuous, with several long climbs and descents. Take food and some water with you (though there are fountains in the villages). In addition to the customary yellow arrows this route has been waymarked recently as the 'Camino de los franceses', with large wooden signposts from time to time. Start as early as possible from Villafranca, especially as the first 5–6km are on a minor road and navigation is not difficult in partial daylight.

This is not just an attractive alternative to the main Camino francés, *however, but a route used by pilgrims in the past, particularly those who were ill or with infectious diseases. The former monastery of San Fructuoso in Villar de Corrales (only the church remains today) is said to have looked after pilgrims and have been on the site of a spring with healing properties.*

Leave Villafranca by the method described for the other two options (page 140), cross a *second* bridge (L, over the **Río Valcarce**) and KSO along the **Calle Salvador** to the NVI at the entrance to the road tunnel *(bar at crossroads)*.

Cross the NVI and KSO ahead (marked 'LE622 Corullón') and then fork R steeply uphill 300m later up minor tarred road marked 'Dragonte 4.3'. KSO, steadily uphill all the time, ignoring turnings. About 1km before the village KSO(R) at fork and reach...

7km Dragonte 900m

KSO through village *(picnic area at end on L and fountain further on on R)*.

When tarmac stops KSO, ignoring first RH turn and after 2km fork R up sign-posted track ('Camino de los franceses, GR11'), passing to RH side of 'bump' in front of you (road is about to bend L). Reach a minor road 1km later and turn L along it. About 300–400m later track joins from back L. KSO downhill to...

4km Moral de Valcarce

Chestnut grove at entrance a good place for a rest. Fountain at end of village.

Continue through village, downhill all the time, and at end fork L downhill by *lavadero*, very steeply down lane with concrete surface (and striations). Descend steeply, zigzagging down through chestnut woods on clear track to valley bottom.

Village of Villar de Corrales and church visible high above on the skyline.

Pass old watermill building (on your L), after which *camino* and stream coincide for a short distance. Continue ahead on clear track through more chestnut woods *(plenty of shade)*, zigzagging your way uphill till you emerge by the church of **San Fructuoso** in village of...

5km Villar de Corrales 1050m

The church originally formed part of a monastery which looked after sick pilgrims, its emplacement visible on wall behind church (all that is left of large complex). Fountain 50m later on L.

Continue uphill on minor road, passing farm (R), and at second fountain (on L) fork R uphill (signpost), up shady walled lane to top of hill (KSO(L) at fork near top) veering R as you climb.

KSO(L) at fork and KSO ahead at crossing at top of hill. KSO ahead along the level *(good views)*, then descend, zigzagging down past old quarry workings. Fork L and then, at next fork, KSO(R).

You can now see San Fiz do Seo, where you are going next, on the other side of the road, slightly above it.

Make your way down through quarry as best you can, heading for San Fiz de Seo and road when they come into view.

Reach road *(sign pointing in opposite direction says 'Ruta Verde' and 'Ruta Wolfram')*. Turn R on road and then 400m later fork L uphill up lane (signposted 'Camino de los franceses') to village of…

7km San Fiz do Seo 650m

Continue uphill towards church and then turn hard L there. KSO at fork, then KSO(L) to end of village where street stops and lane begins. Follow it as it winds its way along the hillside on the level *(quarry visible away to L on other side of road)*.

About 2km after San Fiz KSO(L) at fork then descend gradually, cross stream and KSO on other side (fork L). KSO(R) at fork and continue uphill through chestnut woods *(village of Moldes visible high above you to L on hillside opposite)*. When you come to a T-junction in woods, just below Villasinde, 'Ruta Verde GR1' turns L *down*hill here and you go R, *up*hill, veering L to emerge on road in…

4km Villasinde
Bar (not always open), fountain.

Here you can choose between a) continuing ahead to Herrerías (4km) or b) going down to Vega de Valcarce (2km, for example to sleep). For Vega de Valcarce turn R along road on entering village. At bend by cemetery fork R off road and then turn L immediately down clear lane at side of road. This leads you (waymarked) downhill into **Vega de Valcarce**, turning L and L again and then R at the bottom to cross the **Puente Viejo**. Turn L on main road to rejoin main *Camino francés.*

To continue to Herrerías: on reaching the road in Villasinde cross over, go up short street, turn L at top and KSO, passing to L of church. Fork L at end, veer R and then KSO(R) at fork uphill. Follow road for 1km and then KSO(R) at fork. *(First TV antenna on L uphill.)*

Pass *fountain* on L after 1km and then 500m later turn L downhill off road, very steeply, 150m before a *very* large rock and red-and-white TV masts (500m

146

after fountain). Continue steeply down old track for 1km, veering R near valley bottom. Turn R by bridge in **Herrerías** and then L along road to rejoin the main *Camino francés* in…

♨ 3km Herrerías 680m (610/168)

Shop on road, 2 bars with food.
    The last houses in this village were known as Hospital Inglés, where there was also a chapel where pilgrims who died en route were buried.

As the ground is often very wet here many people in the village wear wooden clogs over their shoes in bad weather, each foot raised up off the ground on three 'legs'.
    Follow road through village then, at a T-junction (signposted to the L to 'San Julian 2'), KSO(R). At the end of the houses there is a L turn marked 'Lindoso 2'; ignore this and KSO(R) here to 'La Faba'.
    Keep R along road and after crossing the second bridge go uphill for 1.5km. Then, at *two* milestone-type marker posts *(one for walkers, the other for cyclists, La Faba visible ahead to L on clear day)* fork L off the road down a FP to the valley floor.
    (If the weather is bad or very wet walkers are recommmended to continue on the cyclist's route, a minor road with very little traffic, then an unsurfaced road, going directly to **Laguna de Castilla** *[so missing out La Faba] and from there to O Cebreiro – waymarked and easy to follow.)*
    A clear rocky track then zigzags its way steeply uphill through chestnut woods. At a junction by a pair of iron gates on L turn *hard* R uphill (**Calle Santiago**) in a straight line, ignoring turnings, and enter the village of…

♨ 3.5km La Faba 917m (613.5/164.5)

Bar (simple meals) summer only, church, *refugio*, three fountains.

Fork L uphill at fountain and continue through village, ignoring turnings to L and R. KSO uphill at end, up shaded lane. Fork R when lane comes out into the open and then KSO uphill along green lane to village of…

2km Laguna de Castilla 1098m (615.5/162.5)

Fountain.

Just outside the village you will see the first of the Galician marker stones: according to this it is 153km to Santiago, though the distance given is somewhat optimistic. These stones, bearing the scallop shell motif, are somewhat like old-fashioned milestones, placed at 500m intervals along the route from now on. They are useful not merely to tell you how many more kilometres you still have left, or to reassure you that you aren't lost (particularly as the camino frequently picks its way through a veritable maze of old lanes and tracks, with constant changes of direction) but also to give you the names of the places you are in, as many of the villages are far too small to have name boards. Galicia is riddled with green lanes, none of which have signposts, so these marker stones are very useful. In the province of La Coruña they are also used as waymarks and have arrows on them to indicate changes of direction, whether or not they coincide with the usual 500m sitings.

Unlike Navarre and Castille-León, where the villages are bigger but very widely spaced, those in Galicia are often extremely small but very close to one another; you are not usually far from a building of some sort.

KSO through village, ignoring turns to L and R.

After 1km you enter Galicia, in the province of *Lugo (large marker stone to R of camino)*. Then, after a further 1km, past a wall with a wood above it (R) and a large stone barn (R) you emerge onto the road at...

Marker stone, entry to Galicia (below O Cebreiro)   (Photo: Ysabel Halpin)

Landscape on way up to O Cebreiro (Photo: Ysabel Halpin)

🏠 2.5km O Cebreiro 1300m (618/160)

Various *fondas* and *mesones* (meals and accommodation), large *refugio*, fountain.

National Monument. A tiny village consisting partly of *pallozas*, round thatched dwellings of Celtic origin, one of which is now a small museum. The village originated with the pilgrim route and the Hostal San Giraldo was a hospital from the 11th century to 1854, founded by monks from the French abbey of Saint Gérard de'Aurillac. The church of Santa María contains relics and a 12th-century statue of the Virgin which reputedly inclined its head after a miracle that took place in the 16th century.

Magnificent views all round in good weather. At night, if it is clear, the Milky Way (used by pilgrims in centuries gone by to guide them as they walked ever due west) is easily seen as there are few street or other lights anywhere in sight – a rare chance to see all the stars against a completely black sky. [RJ: take second R facing monument, with Hostal Giraldo to your L.]

Leave on road (LU634) in direction of Samos/Sarria and KSO to hamlet of…

🏠 3km Liñares (621/156)

Méson (rooms), shop, fountain on L.

Village, O Cebreiro (Photo: Ysabel Halpin)

Fork L off road, enter village, pass church and rejoin road at end. Cross over, turn R immediately at crossroads down minor road. Fork L 100m later up rough track which continues // to road and climbs steeply to rejoin it shortly before KM 31.

1km Alto de San Roque 1270m (623.5/154.5)

Chapel of San Roque, panoramic views. Enormous modern statue of St James 'on the move' towards Santiago (with his own stretch of *camino*) on LH side of road.

Take path on RH side of road (by K147 marker post) and KSO. Continue uphill and at K145.5 enter...

☗ 1.5km Hospital da Condesa (626.5/151.5)

Church of Santiago with sword of Santiago on top of tower. As its name indicates, there was originally a pilgrim hospital in this village. *Refugio.*

Fork R into village off road. KSO. *Fountain.* At end of village continue on road for another 400m then fork R to minor road (signposted to 'Sabugos'). Turn L up lane 200m further on, uphill (small hut on R of road). Fork L at junction, join track coming from L and KSO. Pass through hamlet of **Padornelo** (K143, 1275m).

Church tower,
Hospital de Condesa

Emerge onto minor road at church – KSO and when road bends R continue up track that climbs very steeply to…

3km Alto do Poio 1337m (630/148)
Small group of houses with bar/shop, *mesón*. Capilla Santa María.

From here to Triacastela (13km) the route is downhill all the way. After that, and in Galicia in general, the camino is often shaded, so it is cool and pleasant even in the middle of the day, with speckled sunlight. It is, however, often wet and/or misty in this part, especially in the mornings.

Continue on road for 300m, fork R off road onto clear track // to road and continue on it. Just before *Fonfría* another track joins from back R. [RJ: KSO(R).]

3.5km Fonfría 1290m (630/148)
Bar/*mesón* on road.

There was a pilgrim refuge here as early as 1535, which continued to function until the middle of the last century. It offered free 'light, salt, water and two blankets' to the able-bodied, 'bread, an egg and lard' to the sick. The village takes its name from its 'cool fountain'.

151

*Between O Cebreiro and Triacastela
(Photo: Paddy Dillon)*

Continue on old road through village *(house marked 'CL' has rooms)*. At end, KSO(L) ahead on track // to road. Return to road briefly at K137.5 and turn R off it to lane.

Cross minor road 100m later and continue on lane on other side. Ignore turns to L and R and emerge ahead (opposite bus stop) at entrance to...

🕮 2.5km Viduedo (632.5/145.5)

Bar/*mesón* (rooms), another house with rooms. Ermita de San Pedro.

Fork L and L again through hamlet and continue on lane *(with spectacular views to R but spoilt by huge quarry in the middle distance)*.

KSO slightly uphill after K136 and continue on track which wends its way round the side of **Monte Calderon** (K135.5), descending to hamlet of **Filloval** at K133.5. Turn L at telephone pole down lane to L of farm building and 100m later cross road and veer R downhill down lane between banks. KSO(L) at fork 150m later (track joins from back R) [RJ: KSO(R) just before reaching road] and continue to road *(underpass under construction)*. Cross over.

Continue down walled lane 100m later on other side, at entrance to hamlet of **As Pasantes** (K132). Track joins from back L [RJ: KSO(L)]. Continue through village *(house with 'CL' has rooms)*. Fork L at *ermita*, fork L at end of village down walled lane *(note dovecote in field to L)* and KSO downhill to **Ramil**. Continue through hamlet on paved lane. At K130.5 a minor road joins from back R [RJ: KSO(R)]. Continue down, passing *refugio* to L at entrance, into...

🕮 6.5km Triacastela 665m (639/139)

Shop, bars, restaurant, *hostal* and two *fondas*, *refugio*, private *refugio*, bank (CD), bakery.

End of the 11th stage in Aymery Picaud's guide. Church of Santiago with statue of St James as a pilgrim above door and also inside above new altar.

Continue down the main street *(house no 19 was the former pilgrim hospital)* to the T-junction at the end.

Here you can choose between two routes to Sarria: a) turn L, via Samos, on the road for the first 3km or b) turn R, via San Xil, along green lanes, paths and a few minor roads. This is a little shorter but is more strenuous and there are no shops or bars and only one fountain along the way. The two routes join up a few kilometres before Sarria. Which route you choose will probably depend on the weather (the San Xil option can be very muddy if it has been raining) and whether or not you want to visit the monastery at Samos or stay in the village.

Both options are waymarked but only the San Xil route has the milestone-type marker stones.

NB Watch out carefully for waymarking near Triacastela and elsewhere in this region where there are other long-distance walks marked with yellow-and-white French-style balises. Occasionally they overlap with the camino for short sections.

A: ROUTE VIA SAMOS

Turn L in Triacastela (K129.5), pass modern statue of Santiago Peregrino at edge of road *(fountain to L by market hall)*, cross the bridge over the **Río Oríbio** and KSO along road (LU634) in the direction of *Samos* for 3km to **San Cristobo do Real**.

Turn R off road into village at bend in road by bus shelter *(watch out for yellow arrows: not well waymarked here)* and go down street, passing to L of church. Veer L, cross bridge over **Río Oríbio** *(lavadero on L)*, take LH of two streets and KSO to end of village.

Take lower of two lanes and pass to R of cemetery and go up lane under trees. *(Main road is // above L, on other side of valley)*. KSO(R) uphill at fork and KSO(R) again (uphill) at next and KSO on track, undulating, more or less // to river below.

At junction of four tracks *(small stone hut to your R)* KSO(L) ahead *(waterfall below to your L)*, descending, ignoring turnings, to cross bridge over the **Río Oríbio** again.

Continue uphill ahead, veer L uphill at fork and L again at church and cemetery to rejoin minor road in **Renche** *(bar, Santiago Peregrino in reredos on main altar in church)*.

Turn R off road a few yards further on down a very minor tarred road and then R over bridge over **Río Oaga**. Go over second bridge and continue uphill on road, turn L at hairpin in road along street and fork L at end of village along shady lane *(// to river but higher up)*.

KSO on high-level track, ignoring turnings, until you descend to village of **Tredezín**. Pass in front of church *(to your R, porch useful for shade)*, take second L in front of church and veer L through village. Take R fork at end and R again along walled lane *(// to river again)*.

Continue uphill and onto high-level track again. Turn R at fork, L at T-junction steeply downhill *(not very clearly waymarked)*. Cross bridge over **Río Oríbio**, turn R uphill along lane and enter village of **San Martíno**.

Turn L uphill on very minor road, KSO(R) at fork and near top of hill cross minor road and veer R diagonally up small path which becomes walled lane, to emerge on main road to Sarria just past village of *San Martíno. (Bar on road: summer only?)*.

Turn R along road (not waymarked), L 100m later into lay-by by tunnel under road. Fork L into short lane, cross minor road (signposted 'Freixo 4' on main road)

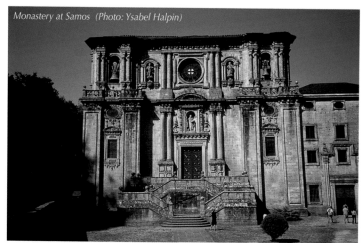
Monastery at Samos (Photo: Ysabel Halpin)

and KSO ahead down lane, downhill between walls to valley bottom. Just *before* bridge over river turn *hard* R into *Samos* down lane which becomes a street, cross bridge *(note wrought-iron railings in shell formation, monastery to your R)* and join main road in middle of village by **Casa do Concello** in...

To leave, continue along the main road towards Sarria (LU632) for 2km. About 300m after the hamlet of **Tequín** with *ermita (dedicated to Santo Domingo de Silos)* fork R very steeply uphill on a minor road marked 'Pascais'.

*This joins the San Xil route at K116 (**Hospital**). It is a little longer than continuing on the road but is shady and much quieter, passing through the countryside on old lanes.*

🏠 11km Samos 532m

Shop, bars, restaurant, two *hostales*, *refugio* at rear of monastery.

Small village dominated by a very large Benedictine monastery (National Monument – guided tours available); this formerly housed some 500 monks but today there are only a handful left.

At the top of the hill, opposite the first building on the R, turn L down lane which then climbs uphill again.

KSO, forking L (lower option) when lane divides. Field track joins from back L; continue along it to a road (100m) and then turn L 50m later at another road, turning L downhill alongside the *12th-century church of* **Santa Eulalia de Pascais** *(church porch a good place for a rest/shelter)*. About 100m later turn R downhill down FP along side of field/wall to join 'U' of horseshoe and take RH fork to valley bottom and then continue uphill up shaded lane.

At fork shortly afterwards *do not* veer round to R uphill again *(river and minor road below you to L)* but take L fork downhill on FP and up and down // to river below. Descend to road, turning R along it for a few metres at a chapel and then fork L down shaded lane // to river but above it.

About 400m later join track coming from above back R and KSO downhill, veering round to R to cross stream. KSO ahead, forking second L at junction 200m later. Join road coming from back L and then follow it round to R. Cross bridge over river and KSO on road. Fork L at bend after second bridge (200m later) at junction marked 'Sivil' and KSO on this road *(river in valley bottom to L)*.

Turn L in village and continue uphill on road and then downhill again. Follow road uphill (it then becomes unsurfaced). Join another road at a 'U' bend and KSO(L) downhill. KSO(R) at next fork and KSO through village and uphill again at end.

Go under road bridge and enter village of **Hospital**, fork L and pass K116. This is where you join the route from San Xil; continue to Sarria as described on page 157.

B: ROUTE VIA SAN XIL

Turn R in Triacastela, cross main road and go along minor road marked 'San Xil'. KSO for 1.5km and then take the *third* of three forks, leading L down green lane to **As Balsas**. KSO through hamlet, cross river and then KSO(R) uphill past farm and *ermita* (on R) through chestnut woods.

Continue till you reach a road, just after K127, with fountain and sitting area, and turn R along it. Reach T-junction 500m later and turn L up to....

4km San Xil (643/135)

Small hamlet with only a few houses.

KSO ahead on road, uphill, passing fountain on R after 1km, until you reach the...

2km Alto de Riocabo (645/133) 896m

Turn R off road here onto a track and KSO, following it round the side of the valley. Pass K123 (**O Real**) and fork L at division of paths. KSO at junction, down hollow, sunken lane, passing K122.5, KSO at next crossing, downhill all the time, to the hamlet of **Montán**, where you turn R between houses. Continue on walled lane. KSO on track that joins from back R. Pass hamlet of **Fontearcuda** and KSO, downhill all the time, down shady lane, until you reach a road. Turn R along it for 100m then, at K122 **Zoo Mondarega** *(Zoo has church of Santiago)* turn hard L downhill down shady track (watch out carefully for the turning). Turn hard R at bottom, veering L and uphill then down until you reach a road at K120.

Turn L along it to **Furela** *(small bar in summer)* and at end of hamlet, after church *(Capilla San Roque)*, fork R. Turn L on road 500m later and KSO, forking R onto a track 200m later. KSO(L) at junction into hamlet of **Pintín** and then turn R down main street. At end of village KSO at bend in road coming from your L *(view of Sarria ahead)*.

Continue on road. Fork R down lane at K117.5. Cross road (church over to L) and continue on FP between trees on other side. Reach road again and continue on its LH side until you reach an island *(refugio in old school on L).*

☎ 8km Calvor (653/125)
Refugio but no other facilities.

KSO then 200m later fork R down road signposted 'Aguiba'. Continue through hamlet of **Hospital** (K116, *so named, like many other such villages, because of its former pilgrim hospital*). KSO at junction with bigger road and veer L along it. KSO on road, pass K115 (**San Mamede**, *just a few houses*) and downhill to Sarria, passing K114.5 (**San Pedro**), K114 (**Carballal**), K113 (**Vigo de Sarria**) until you reach the main Sarria–Samos road at 'stop' sign in the town itself *(bar on R, shortly before junction).*

☎ 4.5km Sarria 420m (657.5/120.5)
All facilities. Several *hostales*, *refugio* in old part of town at Rúa Maior 79.

The old part of the town is up on the hill and includes a modern church dedicated to the Galician martyr Santa Mariña (on the site of a former one), the Romanesque church of El Salvador, the Convento de la Magdalena (originally a pilgrim hospital), the remains of the medieval *castillo* at the top of the hill and several old houses with armorial devices over the doors. Sarria formerly had two other pilgrim hospices too, one in the building on the main street opposite the church (now the courthouse) and another adjoining the Capilla San Lázaro (for pilgrims with leprosy and other contagious complaints).

Sarria to Santiago de Compostela

The section from Sarria to Portomarín is one of the quietest and most peaceful of the camino and, in summer at least, there are several bars along the way that do meals. At other times make sure you have enough food (and water) with you before you leave Sarria as although the route passes through many villages they are all extremely small, with no facilities of any kind until you reach Portomarín.

Cross over and follow the road as it veers round to R, passing K112. Cross bridge over the river **Río Oríbio**, cross main (Monforte–Sarria) road and go up a steep street with steps (the **Escalinata Maior**), veer L and continue uphill almost straight ahead, up the **Rúa Maior**, *(refugio on R)*, passing the church of **El Salvador** on your R *(note modern frescoes outside)*. Pass police station (L), chapel of **Santa Misión** (at top, L) and turn R past the old **Prisión Penetencial** (R) along the **Avenida de la Feria.** Pass market (L) and descend slightly towards the **Mosteiro da Magdalena** (monastery). Turn L downhill beside the cemetery, turn R at bottom by electricity substation and then turn L to cross the medieval **Ponte Aspera** (K110.5).

KSO down a lane to the Madrid–La Coruña railway line. The path continues alongside the track before bending L and then R to become a green lane. Cross railway line (carefully!) at K109.5 (**Sancti Michaelis**) and continue // to the railway line. Cross stream by footbridge and continue uphill through oakwoods, forking L again uphill at fork.

Path zigzags uphill and crosses large field at top. Turn R along track by first farm building at end of wall. Continue to road, turn L and then veer R 100m later (K108, **Vilei**). Follow road through village and continue on road. *Good views to L.* Fork R ahead at fork by small bus shelter and KSO to church (road bends R just before it) in…

🏠 4.5km Barbedelo 580m (662/116)

Refugio in old school on R by playing field (spectator stand a good place for rest/keeping dry if raining).

Romanesque church of Santiago, a National Monument and worth a visit for its frescoes.

Turn R uphill up road by church, veer L at K107 and at the top turn L off the road into a lane at K106.5 (**Rente**). KSO ahead, veer R through village to road coming from back R (*'Casa Turismo Rural del Peregrino' – rooms – on L at bend)* and continue on road, ignoring turns to L and R. KSO, cross another road and veer R 20m behind buildings on road (*do not* turn L to farm) and continue down tree-lined lane.

At K105 [RJ: fork R] pass modern fountain (*with water coming out of 'pelegrin's' mouth, stone sitting area*). Lane joins from back R [RJ: KSO(R)].

Pass K104.5 (**Marzán O Real**) and continue along lane. About 150m later turn R, slightly downhill alongside wall (*Fenosa – electricity company – tower behind it*). Continue along walled lane through woods.

Cross road and KSO on minor road (*bar/*mesón *at junction*). Pass K103.5 at **Leimán**. KSO, veering L at triple fork and continue on road to village of **Peruscallo** (*fountain*).

Here you encounter one of the many hórreos *typical of this region – long narrow rectangular stone or brick storehouses raised up on legs and used for keeping potatoes, corncobs and so on. They have a cross on top of the roof at one end and a decorative knob at the other and vary enormously in size; some are only 2 or 3m long but others may be as long as 15–20m.*

Veer L shortly after K102.5 and continue down walled lane, often flooded, but with raised path along LH side and then stepping stones in centre. Fork L at fork alongside field, pass K102 (**Cortiñas**) and KSO, ignoring turns, to village itself. Join very minor road coming from back R [RJ: KSO(R)]. KSO(L) ahead at fork.

Fork R at next fork (K101.5, **Lavandeira Casal**) along walled lane. Turn R on main road 150m later then immediately L down another walled lane, continue on road at bend coming from your L [RJ: KSO(L)], passing to R of houses.

KSO(R) downhill down walled lane, pass K101 and veer L at bottom and then uphill again (*this section is often flooded in bad weather*). Continue ahead, ignoring turns, pass K100.5 (**Brea**) and continue to minor road. Turn R and then follow road, veering L through village and continue on downhill to village of **Morgade** (K99.5, *bar with rooms, meals, fountain*).

Continue ahead (*deserted* ermita *on RH is useful for a rest if raining*). KSO(L) at fork (downhill) and KSO(R) at next fork (*another section often flooded*). Continue uphill to...

🏠 9km Ferreiros (671/107)
Refugio, bar/restaurant (summer only?) at end of village, fountain.

To go to *refugio* (*white building at end of village on FP*) turn L at entrance to *Ferreiros. Otherwise:* fork R to pass above it on road then continue R ahead to top of hill (bar/restaurant to L). At end of village KSO downhill down minor road (*tower of cemetery chapel visible 50m below you*) to K98 (**Mirallos,** *Romanesque church of Santa María, restaurant to LH side of road*).

159

Continue through **Pena** (K97.5) and veer R and then L in village *(fountain)* and join road coming from back R. [RJ: fork R into village.] KSO on road ignoring turnings.

Continue through **Couto-Rozas** *(fountain)* and turn R off road up walled lane at K96.5 and take L (lower) option at fork 200m later. Pass K96 (**Pena dos Corvos**) and K95.5 (**Moimentos**), cross similar track and continue downhill, veering R to road. Cross river and continue downhill, turn R along another road and 100m later turn L down lane at K95 (**Cotarelo Mercadoiro**) and large cement wayside cross.

KSO down lane ignoring turnings, through village of **Moutras** (K94.5), continue uphill and join road coming from R [RJ: fork R downhill] and KSO(L) on road.

KSO on road at K94. *(After this it is downhill all the way down to Portomarín, 4km.)* Turn L and then R 500m later (K93.5) when road bends round to R and go down lane *(view of reservoir and Portomarín ahead)* to road at K93 (**Parrocha**). Fork L through village to end, join road coming from back R [RJ: KSO(R) at fork] and continue ahead on road for 100m.

Turn R down walled lane at K92.5. Join another lane coming from back R [RJ: fork R uphill up rocky lane] and continue downhill, pass K92 (**Vilachá**) and KSO to road. Cross over, go down short lane and KSO(R) ahead, veering R through village to join road coming from R [RJ: fork R]. Turn L at K91.5 then R and KSO(R) ahead leaving village and KSO to road, ignoring turns to L and R.

Turn R at junction (K91) then second L ahead and L again 50m later, steeply downhill *(bar on R)*. At T-junction below turn L slightly, follow road round and then R at K90. In front of you you will see the **Río Miño** and the **Embalse de Belezar** *(reservoir)*. Cross bridge over the river, turn L along road to continue or go up steep flight of steps ahead and turn R at top to enter...

⌂ 7km Portomarín 550m (678/100)

Shops, bars, restaurant, *hostal*, youth hostel. Large *refugio* with capacious overflow facilities in summer. One of the bakeries in the town is famous for its 'Torta de Santiago', a large plate-size almond tart (extremely filling) decorated with the cross that is a combination of a sword and a shepherd's crook.

The original town was flooded when the river Miño was dammed up to build the reservoir in the early 1960s, and the new town built up on the hill above it. Before this took place, however, the fortified Romanesque church of San Nicolás was taken to pieces stone by stone (the numbers can still be seen today) and rebuilt on its present town centre site. The portal is by Master Mateo (who built the Portico de la Gloria in the Cathedral in Santiago). The other church in Portomarín, San Pedro, is also Romanesque.

There are several kilometres of road walking in this next stretch (and 14km steadily uphill as far as Sierra de Ligonde) but there is not usually too much traffic.

To leave Portomarín: after turning L on other side of bridge pass in front of petrol station and turn L either over the new road bridge (signed 'Club Nautico') or 50m further on via the old footbridge. Turn R on other side up minor road and fork L 100m later uphill at K89 up shady lane.

After 1.5km, near top of hill, cross minor road leading to *San Mamed(e) Belad(e)* and continue on path // to old main road, C535, behind bus shelter. Pass to R of factory and cross road (K87) to continue on wide track on RH side of road.

Cross over to LH side 1.5km later, opposite the *Bima (cattle-food) factory* and continue on track // to road at K85.5 (**Toxibo**). At junction with main road turn L 150m later, continue ahead up lane passing behind houses and // to road but not immediately adjoining. Take L fork at fork [RJ: fork L].

At junction with another lane coming from L turn R shortly after K84 to return to road and track alongside it (LH side), continuing to…

⚓ 7.5km Gonzar (685.5/92.5)

Small village with Romanesque church of Santa María and *refugio* in old school by road. Bar on road (summer only) does simple meals.

Turn L 20m after *refugio* and bus shelter along lane and then turn R to continue on unsurfaced track, // to road but away from it. Continue, ignoring turns, to road coming from R at entrance to village and turn L along it.

⚓ 1km Castromaior (686.5/91.5)

Bar; white house to L in centre has rooms.

Veer L and then R along road through village (uphill) and KSO uphill at end to main road at K80. Turn L along path // to road [RJ: fork R off main road at minor road signed 'Castromaior'] and continue (still uphill!) L on road, crossing to continue on RH side after 300m.

KSO and then cross back to LH side shortly after K79 and fork L along unsurfaced road. Pass K78.5 and reach…

⚓ 2.5km Hospital de la Cruz (689/89)

Refugio in old school on L at end of village. Bar/restaurant. Site of former pilgrim hospice.

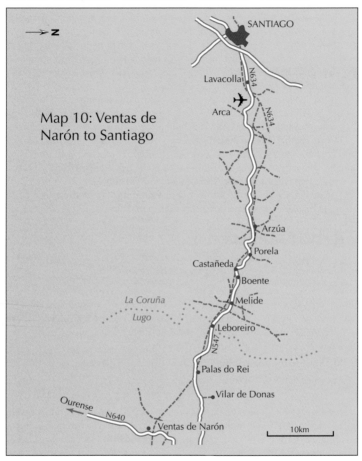

Map 10: Ventas de
Narón to Santiago

Cross similar type of track and continue down lane to village itself *(bar in summer)*.
　　Fork L at end past *refugio* (in old school) to main road and cross it via FB. Go
uphill and then turn L at K78 on old road and KSO through village of…

1.5km Ventas de Narón (690.5/87.5)

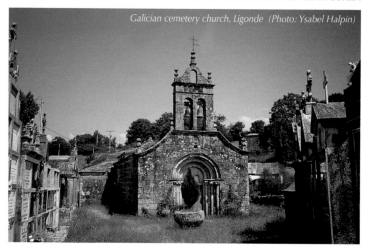
Galician cemetery church, Ligonde (Photo: Ysabel Halpin)

Pass to R of *chapel* (K77) and wooden wayside cross *(bar, picnic area)* and continue (still uphill...) on road until you pass K76.5, **Sierra de Ligonde** at 756m *(panoramic views on a clear day)*, after which the road descends. KSO, ignoring turnings. Road joins from back L [RJ: KSO(L) uphill] and continue downhill. Pass K75 (**Previsa**) and K74.5 (**Lameiro**).

Note chapel to R of road and then, 200m later on L by enormous tree – good place for a rest – an interesting wayside cross with a skull on its base.

Enter village of...

⌂ 3km Ligonde (693.5/83.5)

Refugio in summer months run by a religious organisation. Fountain.
  Site of a pilgrim hospice in former times with pilgrim cemetery still in place.

Continue to end of village, passing stone cross on top of wall (R), veering R and then L down to cross bridge over river. Continue ahead uphill *(bar R in summer)* to...

⌂ 4.5km Eirexe (Airexe) (698/80)

Bar at entrance, *refugio* in old school on RH side of road in centre.
  The village takes its name from the Galician word for 'church' (and this

one has a Romanesque portal with sculpture of Daniel and animals on south wall and a statue of Santiago Peregrino inside).

KSO(L) at fork in village. Pass *lavadero* and fountain (on L) and continue to a crossroads at **As Cruces** (K72). KSO ahead down road marked 'Palas de Rey 10'. Pass through hamlet of **Portos, Vilar de Donas** (K71, *bar with meals*).

*(From here a detour of 3km [each way] is recommended, along a lane to R, to **Vilar de Donas** with its Romanesque church of El Salvador, a National Monument, with 14th-century wall paintings and effigies of the Knights of the Order of Santiago who took it over in 1184. Turn R shortly after last* hórreo *in village [signposted].)*

Pass through hamlet of **Lestedo** (K70.5), veer R uphill at *lavadero*, passing its church of St James and wayside cross (K70). Continue uphill straight on through hamlet of **Valos (Balos)** (K69.5), ignoring turns to L and R. Continue on road, passing K69 (**Remollón Mamurria**).

KSO ahead, ignoring turns to L and R and KSO(L) ahead behind house along track // to main road. Pass K68 (**Ave Nostre/Lamelas**) *(mesón)*, cross lane and KSO, passing K67.5 (**Alto do Rosario**), till you join main (N547) road at junction with a minor road coming from your L (at road KM 32).

Continue on FP to L of road for 250m then turn L down paved lane between buildings at K67 (**O Rosario**, *a cluster of houses*) by bus shelter. Continue downhill, passing to R of sports centre *(fountain opposite)* and KSO ahead at K66.5. Veer R on road past shop (on your L), veer second R and go down steps past church (K65.5). Turn R into the street and then cross main street in town of…

🏠 **7km Palas do Rei 565m (705/73)**

Small town with all facilities but no very interesting features. Four *hostales/fondas*, large *refugio* in centre.

End of the 12th stage in Aymery Picaud's guide and the start of the 13th, the last, to Santiago.

To leave: go down more steps (**Traversia de la Iglesia**), down street to R of *Correos/Ayuntamiento*, pass fountain and modern statue of Santiago Peregrino and cross over. Go on lower section of old road (alongside main road but *inside* crash barrier).

Go uphill and at K64 (**Carballal**) turn RT up walled lane uphill. At top veer L when it levels out, then R, to return to main road at top of the hill. Cross over and continue on FP behind crash barrier (LH side) then at bend 60m later KSO and then turn L down hollow lane at K63.5, continuously downhill. KSO, pass K63 **A Laguna** and continue on lane to minor road coming from back L [RJ: fork L uphill]. About 20m later KSO(L) down another lane. KSO(L) at K62.5 (**San Xulian do Camino**) and continue downhill to road. Turn L along it, continue through village and pass to R of *hórreo* and church and KSO.

Pass K62 (**Pallota**) and continue on road to T-junction and then continue down lane ahead. At road at bottom turn L, cross bridge over river, turn R up lane (paved to begin with) and then L uphill (K61) up lane. Continue through woods. KSO when minor road joins from L and again shortly afterwards when road joins from back R [RJ: fork R]. Pass K60 in hamlet of...

♜ 5.5km Casanova (710.5/67.5)

Refugio in old school on R.

Fork L uphill, then L down lane (K59.9). KSO(R) at next fork (after K59) and continue downhill, pass K58.5 (**Porto de Bois**) and KSO to cross bridge over stream. Unsurfaced track joins from back R (K58 **Campanilla**) [RJ: fork R] and then from back L 50m later [RJ: KSO(L)].

Join main road coming from back L [RJ: fork L onto track] just before K57.5 (**Coto**) and continue. Enter the province of *La Coruña* at next (minor) road junction.

Here the milestones, normally on your R, are not only at 500m intervals but are also used, with appropriate arrows, to indicate changes of direction. [RJ: they will therefore be on your L – facing away from you.]

Continue for a short distance to the main road (N547), signposted 'Santiago 60, Melide 6'. Turn L at junction [RJ: turn R down minor road signposted 'Pedruzo'] *(bar/shop on L, hostal/restaurant to R)* and then turn L off main road after 100m along a track, passing near *refugio (Melide now visible ahead)* leading to village of...

♜ 3.5km Leboreiro (714/64)

Refugio on outskirts of village, fountain. Simple Romanesque church of Santa María (the building opposite was the former pilgrim hospital), *rollo*.

Continue through village on paved street, cross reconstructed copy of old bridge over the **Río Seco** and continue ahead along lane // to main road (over to your R), ignoring turns. Pass K56 (**Disicabo**) and fork R behind factory (K55.5, **Magdalena**). KSO and then turn L at K55 along tree-lined track // to main road for 2km.

This track winds about quite a bit as it follows the outline of a new business park, Parque Empresarial de Melide. Originally the camino was on the main road so this is a safer (though no prettier) alternative.

About 100m after K53.5 turn L at road KM 48 and veer R behind a factory along the edge of eucalyptus woods. Continue ahead on road at junction and then fork R 200m later (downhill). Turn L (K52.5) at bottom, then R over bridge over the **Río Furelos** in the village of **Furelos** itself *(which formerly had a pilgrim hospice)*. Turn L at end on paved road, pass church *(simple bar on L)* and turn L again through village. At end turn R onto unsurfaced track (K52), planted with young trees.

KSO ignoring turns, continue on paved lane, fork R at end (K51 **Melide**) and 20m later enter main street (**Avenida de Lugo**) [by cycle/moto shop for RJ].

> **🐚 6km Melide   454m (720/58)**
>
> All facilities. *Hostal* and two *fondas*. Large *refugio* on leaving town (near church of Santa María).
>
>   Pleasant small town with public garden in centre, several 'pulperías' (stalls or restaurants serving squid). Churches of San Pedro, Sancti Spiritu (former monastery church, with pilgrim hospital opposite) and, up on the hill as you leave the town, the Romanesque church of Santa María.

Continue along main street past public garden (L) and turn R at large ornate *fountain* at junction and then turn L along the **Rúa San Pedro** and its continuation the **Rúa Principal**. *(Another fountain in small square to R.)* Pass church of **Santa María** (L) and cemetery (L), both at the top of the hill, and KSO downhill along lane to road at the bottom. Cross it and enter hamlet of **Santa María** *(shop, bar).* [RJ: cross road and go up lane veering R.]

Turn R 200m further on down paved road, past a chapel and another cemetery. *Here you encounter the first of the many eucalyptus woods you will meet from now on. From here too, until the outskirts of Santiago, the route leads in and out of the woods most of the time so that although the temperature may be quite high in summer walking is still very pleasant as much of the route is shaded.*

Continue on gravelled lane // to main road (150m or more to your R), ignoring turns to R. Pass K49.5 (**Carballal**).

KSO(R) at junction shortly after electricity substation (K49) on your L and enter eucalyptus woods. Continue downhill, KSO(L) at fork (K48.5), cross river at bottom by FB and KSO uphill again.

Turn L at junction and continue uphill, veering R [track from back L, RJ]. KSO(L) then turn L again to emerge on main road by bus shelter at road KM 52

(K47.5 **Raído**). Continue on FP on LH side of road for 100m then turn L (by phone box) down unsurfaced road which veers R to continue through woods.

KSO on forest road, pass **Parabispo** (K46.8), ignore all turns and continue in more or less a straight line, // to main road away to your R. Go downhill, veer L out of woods to fields. Cross stream (K46, boundary of *Concello de Arzúa*) and KSO on unsurfaced road with young trees on either side. Ignore all turns, pass **Peroxa** (K45.5), KSO(L) at junction at entry to...

5.5km Boente (725.5/52.5)

Bar on road. Fountain at crossing, *rollo*, church of Santiago, restored in 1994, with statues of Santiago Peregrino (main altar), Santiago Matamoros (above main door) and San Roque (to RH side of main altar).

Turn R in village and veer L *(fountain)* to rejoin road at wayside cross and *fountain*. Turn R at church and then L straight away and KSO down track to road (K44.5), cross it and continue downhill towards the **Río Boente.** Go *under* main road and after crossing river lane veers L to climb steeply uphill to road at road bridge at top of hill (K43.5, road KM 56).

KSO(L) along road, pass K43 (**Castañedra**) and KSO. After 300m turn L on minor road signposted to 'Rio Pomar Doroña' *(bar/shop 200m ahead to RH side of old main road)* then KSO(R) 50m later at junction. Pass K42.5 (**Pedrido**). Continue downhill to **Río** (K42), veer L to cross bridge over stream and continue uphill again.

KSO at next crossing (// to main road) and continue uphill again (steep). Cross minor road and continue uphill (yet) again. Enter eucalyptus woods, veer diagonally R to top of hill and then L downhill. About 10m after K40.5 the *camino* crosses a bridge over a new road in a very steep cutting. KSO ahead on path through woods on other side. Cross minor road *(bar on L)* and KSO downhill, crossing the bridge over the river **Río Iso** at the bottom in the village of...

♨ 5.5km Ribadiso de Baixo (731/47)

The first house on the R by the river, a pilgrim hospice in medieval times, has now been restored as a *refugio*.

Continue uphill, turn diagonally L at junction 300m later, continue to main road above (K39), ignoring confusing marker stone to L below road.

Watch out carefully here as there are yellow-and-white waymarks for another walk that passes through this area. [RJ: turn L down road signposted to 'Rendal'.] Join (new) main road after bend and continue on road to...

🏠 3km Arzúa 389m (734/44)

Small town with all facilities, several *fondas, refugio.*
   Churches of Santa María (parish church) and La Magdalena (former Augustinian convent with a pilgrim hospital).

Continue into town and then fork L (behind the *Hostal Teodora*) into the **Rúa Cima do Lugar**, // to main road and KSO. Pass church of **Santa María** (R), go down **Rúa do Carmen**, cross another street and KSO. Fork L (K36.5) just before a factory, down a paved lane and KSO.

   Pass K36 (**As Barrosas**), cross track and KSO. Pass **Ermita de San Lázaro** *(L, now in private hands)*. Turn L at junction at top of hill (main road is now 150m to your R) along unsurfaced road which then veers round to R, downhill to valley bottom. Veer L, track joins from back L [RJ: KSO(L) ahead].

   Cross stream and then climb steeply uphill again. Turn L at top along minor road coming from R (this is the **Rúa de Preguntoño**), pass small restored building with 'Lugar de Preguntoño' in tiles above the door and KSO(R) at fork: *ignore the 'wrong direction' crossed yellow-and-white balises in front of you belonging to a local waymarked walk. (No yellow arrow here.)* Cross minor road 20m later and continue uphill opposite. Go under main road and turn L and then R on other side, steeply uphill. Continue on fairly level lane ahead which then climbs slightly uphill again between fields, veering L after 200m or so.

   This is not as complicated as it may sound as you are merely 'playing hide and seek' with the main road, now on your LH side. The marker stones in this area have no distances on them for a while as the route has been altered to take the camino off the road and it is therefore slightly longer than before.

   Cross minor road and continue ahead (the track you are on becomes a road after the crossing). *Arzúa visible behind you.* Fork L along lane 200m later in hamlet and L again 50m further on along track through woods and then downhill.

   Turn R downhill at fork and KSO, ignoring turns, till you reach a minor (tarred) road. Turn L up it, steeply uphill (K33 to your L). At slightly staggered junction at top of hill (K32.5) KSO ahead, still uphill.

   Track joins from back R at K32 (**Tabernavella**) [RJ: fork R]. KSO ahead past next L turn, enter woods again and go slightly downhill again at junction (K31.5).

   KSO ahead at K31 (**Calzada**), cross minor road and KSO ahead all the time, ignoring all turnings. *(Road away to your L, // to camino.)* At junction with minor road (unsurfaced) coming from back L by houses shortly after K29.5 KSO(L) to L of farm buildings [RJ: KSO(R) uphill on track up lane] and rejoin track a few metres later. Turn second R at K29.2 (**Calle**).

   About 20m later go down muddy paved lane between houses *under a hórreo.*

At bend in road at bottom KSO then turn L 20m later at junction. Turn R 50m later down lane under vines. Cross stream by stone boulder footbridge (unstable), cross road and turn first R on other side between buildings then L on minor road. About 20m later fork R up walled lane (at junction with another minor road coming from back L) and after 100m cross minor road and KSO uphill on gravelled road.

If the green lane is flooded in bad weather do not fork R but KSO ahead, turning R at minor road crossing and then immediately L uphill.

KSO, cross another minor road, continue ahead on road marked 'Suso' and turn L 60m later (at K28) up smaller tarred road passing cluster of houses at **Boavista** (K27.8). *(The main road is parallel for much of this section so, once again, it is not as complicated as it may seem.)* At next minor road *do not* KSO but turn L and then immediately R under trees (a 'staggered' junction). Join minor road *(leading to white house on your R – K27)*, cross road and KSO slightly uphill to woods again. KSO.

Pass K26.3 (**Salceda**), cross a minor road, continue ahead for 50m, fork L at fork, pass K26 and veer L to rejoin main road by road place-name sign for...

11km Salceda (745/33)
Bar/shop.

Turn R along main road for 200m [RJ: turn L down lane after last house on L after bar] then fork R up lane *(another bar ahead on main road).*

Pass memorial (R) to Guillermo Watt, a pilgrim, aged 69, who died there on 25 August 1993, one day short of Santiago: a bronze sculpture of a pair of shoes set in a niche in a curved dry-stone wall.

Cross minor road, pass K25 and rejoin main road.

About 100m later cross over and fork L along forest track // to road. Pass K24.5 (**Xen**), cross road, KSO downhill down track, pass K24 (**Ras**), rejoining main road again in hamlet itself.

Cross over main road and continue on lane on other side. KSO(L) at junction. Pass K23.5 (**Brea**) and *memorial stone to Mariano Sánchez-Coursa Carro, a pilgrim on foot who died here on 24 September 1993.* KSO, turn L at minor road and then R down wide lane. KSO to a farm (K23, **Rabiña**), fork L (farm on R). Turn L at junction and rejoin main road. [RJ: turn L down minor road marked 'Rabiña/Arnal'.] Turn R along road. Continue along this for 1km and at **Empalme** at top of hill turn R to minor road *(bar/café, shop, restaurant).* Turn L 100m later by bus shelter along side of woods (K21.5). Emerge on main road at K21, continue on track alongside it (RH side) for a few yards and then go under the road if you want to visit the chapel of...

♠ 5km Santa Irene (750/28)

Two *refugios*, one private (on LH side of road, meals for those staying there), the other (on RH side, part of the network run by the Xunta de Galicia).

Return by tunnel and continue on RH side of main road, pass K20.5 (**Santa Irene**) and *refugio* at side of road by junction with minor road to *Leborán*. Fork R downhill onto gravel track into woods, cross road (carefully) after 300m and turn L down a track and veer R after wood yard (K19.5) to woods. KSO.

At minor road (join it at bend – *bar 100m to R on main road*) KSO (**Rua** K19). Ignore turns and KSO to main road again after K18.5. Cross it and KSO on other side up lane to eucalyptus woods. Ignore turns to L and R and KSO through woods till you come out at the side of a very large hangar/warehouse (on the R). Turn R in front of it along tarmac road and past school sports ground. Pass K17.5 (**Pedrouzo**) at the end.

♠ 3km Arca (Pedrouzo) (758/20)

Shop, pharmacy, bank, bar/restaurants, large *refugio* on main road.

To enter the village turn L after stadium. To continue on the *camino* turn R and then L (after *bar* on L) into woods again.

Turn L at the end onto a minor road (K16.9 **San Antón**). Turn L and KSO(R) and after 100m fork L to return to woods again at K16.5. Fork R (KSO) at fork after 300m, pass K16, turn L at end of woods and immediately R along track between fields, // to road. Turn L 300m later, then R after 100m on minor road. Pass K15 and at bottom of hill turn R in village of...

2.5km Amenal (760.5/17.5)

Bar/tabac. Small supermarket 200m further on on (L) main road.

Fork L, cross river, cross main road (carefully) and continue up steep lane between buildings. Cross road and continue on other side (K14, **Cimadevila**) up lane into woods. Track joins from back R. [RJ: fork L.] About 300m later cross track and fork L diagonally uphill and KSO, ignoring turns, uphill for 1km.

At T-junction at top *(Santiago airport is behind the trees ahead)* turn R (K12.5) down forest lane for 300m to main road (K12).

After this the kilometre marker posts with the distances remaining to Santiago have been re-set and K12 becomes K15,087.

Eucalyptus woods, Galicia (Photo: Paddy Dillon)

Turn L down clear FP between road (on R) and airport perimeter fence (on L). Pass behind airport observation platform and 200m later rejoin main road (N634). Cross over and turn L alongside it on FP under pergolas and 250m later turn R down minor road to small hamlet of **San Paio** *(restaurant)*. Turn L at church *(Santa Lucia de Sabugueira)*, follow road round up *very* steep hill and fork R at top onto track leading into woods (// to road to begin with).

At crossing with similar tracks turn L to Lavacolla and KSO for 1km, following lane which then joins a minor road coming from back L [RJ: fork L at house no 28] and KSO into village of…

☎ 7.5km Lavacolla (768/10)

Hostal, bars, shop. The only fountain is 100m up lane off main road (to L, signposted 'Fonte de Labacolla') opposite bar San Miguel (after chapel), down some steps to L of lane.

Small village where, traditionally, pilgrims washed in the river and generally made themselves presentable before entering Santiago.

The original camino *went past the* **Capilla San Roque**, *on RH side of what is now the main road (good picnic spot, shady).* If you want to do this continue on the road for 3.5km to road KM 717 and then, after passing **Fundación Sotelo Blanco: Museo de Antropoloxia** (on RH side of main road) cross road, go along gravel path towards huge 'Monte de Gozo' sign by school and turn R along the **Rúa San Marcos**. *(Quicker, but there is a lot of traffic.)*

Otherwise, turn L to main road below parish church in Labacolla (temporarily *away from* Santiago), go along it for 100m and then cross it *(shop)* and turn R along minor road signposted to 'Vilamaior'. This takes you along quiet roads more or less // to the main road.

Follow road round to R and KSO to village of **Vilamaior** (2km). Turn L in village and then R. KSO. When you get to a junction (after 2km) with a *campsite* to your L turn L past one TV station *(Televisión de Galicia)* and then R after another TV station *(TVE)*.

Turn R at junction and then L immediately afterwards down **Rúa de San Marcos**. KSO until you reach the **Capilla San Marcos** and the...

Sculpture, Monte de Gozo

☎ 6km Monte del Gozo (Monxoi) 368m (774/4)

A very large modern sculpture marks the place from where pilgrims could see the Cathedral of Santiago for the first time after their long journey, and which was thus known as the 'Mount Joy'. It was formerly a quiet green hill, but at the time of the Pope's visit to Santiago in 1989 it was levelled to make room for the vast crowds there for an open-air mass. The area just below it is now covered with a large complex of accommodation (for 3000 people), amphitheatre, car parks and restaurants, resembling a cross between a military barracks and a holiday camp. Pilgrims with a *credencial* can stay here (free of charge for one night only, after that there is a charge). Useful if you arrive here late in the day so that you can complete the final stage in a leisurely way the following morning.

The chapel of San Marcos is surrounded by trees and is a good place for a picnic or final rest.

Continue on past chapel, downhill. When you get to the bottom, just before the main road and just past a house (L) *with two stone rollos in its garden and a lot of very large concrete animals (dinosaurs and the like)* go down a flight of steps to L and cross bridge over motorway. *(Like the entry to many cities, the out-skirts of Santiago are not very inviting.)*

2km San Lázaro (776/2)

Suburb of Santiago.

After crossing the motorway KSO along the **Rúa do Valiño** (the road you are already on) passing the church of **San Lázaro** *(bars and so on)*. Fork L off the main road down the **Rúa do Valiño,** continuing as **Barrio das Fontiñas** when you see a very large modern housing complex to the L below the road. When you reach a big junction with traffic lights (the *Avenida de Lugo* L goes to the new town) continue uphill along the **Barrio de los Concheiros.**

After passing a small square (L) with the cross of the *Homo Sancto* the road becomes the **Rúa San Pedro.** Follow this down to the **Porto do Camiño**, the traditional pilgrim entry point, then go up the **Rúa das Casas Reales**, cross the **Plaza de Parga**, the **Plaza de Animas**, turn L into the **Plaza Cervantes** and then R down the **Calle Azabachería** to the Cathedral. Go round to the front, in the huge **Plaza de Obradoiro** and enter the Cathedral by the **Portico de la Gloria.**

☖ 2km Santiago de Compostela 264m (778/0)

Population 80,000. All facilities. RENFE. Accommodation in all price ranges. *Refugio* in Seminario Menor (check availability). Two campsites: one on the main road to La Coruña, the other at As Cancelas (on outskirts). Tourist Office: 43 Rúa do Vilar (near Cathedral).

The most important of the many places of interest in Santiago (all in the old town) is the Cathedral, part Romanesque, part Baroque, with its magnificent Portico de la Gloria and façade giving onto the Plaza del Obradoiro. The Cathedral also houses what is probably the world's biggest censer (incense burner), the famous 'Botafumeiro'. It is made of silver and weighs nearly 80kg, requiring a team of eight men and a system of pulleys to set it in motion after mass, swinging at ceiling level from one end of the transept to the other. Guidebooks (in English) are available from the bookshops in the Rúa do Villar (near the Cathedral) or in the new town (for example, Follas Novas, Calle Montero Ríos 37). Try to spend two or three days in Santiago, as there is much to see and do.

If you have time two pilgrim destinations outside the city are worth visiting. **Padrón** is where the boat bringing St James to Galicia is believed to have arrived in AD44, and also contains the museum of Rosalía de Castro, the 19th-century Galician poet; it can be reached easily by bus (some 20km) from Santiago bus station. **Finisterre**, the end of the known world in former times and the end of the route for many pilgrims in centuries gone by, can be reached by bus (95km) from Santiago bus station (daily). If you prefer, however, you can continue there on foot – a three-day journey described below.

Main altar, Santiago Cathedral (Photo: Ysabel Halpin)

Santiago de Compostela to Finisterre

Finisterre ('Fisterra' in Galician) was the end of the known world until Columbus altered things, and was the final destination for many of the pilgrims who made the journey to Santiago in centuries gone by. There are various explanations as to how this continuation came about (one is that it was based on a pre-Christian route to the pagan temple of Ara Solis in Finisterre, erected to honour the sun), but it is also known that a pilgrim infrastructure existed, with 'hospitals' in Cée, Corcubión, Finisterre itself and elsewhere. There are also several pilgrim references along the way: a *cruceiro* with a figure of Santiago in the village of Trasmonte; the church of Santiago in Olveiroa, with a statue of St James; probable pilgrim hospital in the place of that name (apart from those already mentioned in Cée and Corcubión); the church of Santiago at Ameixenda, 2km south of Cée, with a relic reputed to be of one of St James's fingers; a large statue of San Roque in pilgrim gear in the church of San Marcos in Corcubión; a statue of St James in the church of Santa María das Areas in Finisterre with a cemetery chapel that formerly belonged to its pilgrim hospital; and two references to San Roque in place names: the **encrucijada** or **alto de San Roque** at the top of the hill leaving Corcubión and the *San Roque* area at the entrance to Finisterre. And after pilgrims' accounts of their journeys along the *Camino francés*, the route most frequently written about in the past was the continuation to Finisterre/Muxia. These came from various European countries and were in several different languages, including that by the 17th-century Italian Domenico Laffi, four times a pilgrim to Santiago, who describes his visit to the church of Santa María das Areas, 2km before the 'end of the earth' itself.

It is still possible to walk there avoiding main roads but, although numbers have increased considerably in the last few years, only a very small percentage of those who make the pilgrimage to Santiago continue on to Finisterre. This has no doubt been in part due to lack of information and route-finding difficulties, but now that the entire route has been re-waymarked those who feel their journey would be incomplete without continuing to the 'end' will find it easy to do so. Pilgrims in the past also continued to the **Santuario de Nuestra Señora de la Barca** in **Muxia**, 22km further up the Atlantic coast, to the north of Finisterre. This route has also been waymarked recently but is not described here. Anyone interested in walking this continuation to Muxia will find a short guide (in Spanish) in a supplement (No 47) to the February 1996 issue of *Peregrino* magazine, and in the Xunta de Galicia's recent booklet *Camino de Santiago en Galicia: Camino de Fisterra–Muxia*, available from their Oficina do Camiño in the Avenida de Coruña in Santiago (near the Santa Susanna park).

The **route** described here leads 75km due west from Santiago, in roughly a straight line, along footpaths, quiet roads and country lanes. You may have to be more alert to route-finding than you needed to be on the *Camino francés* but continuing to the coast on foot is definitely worth the effort. Finisterre is the real end of the journey, both in the physical sense and in the religious and historical one. You will pass a number of interesting small churches, *pazos* (large Galician country houses) and old bridges along the way, apart from the familiar *hórreos*, and the scenery is often beautiful. It is very peaceful and, as there are still relatively few walkers, the route is quite different from the often 'motorway-like' *Camino francés* to Santiago in the summer months. It does rain a lot in this part of Spain and it is often misty in the mornings but you will have the opportunity to see something of the real Galicia, away from the big towns.

Allow at least three days to walk to Finisterre, with possible overnight stops in Negreira and Olveiroa, where new *refugios* have been built. The actual walking isn't hard but there are a lot of climbs and descents. The route is **waymarked** with the familiar yellow arrows and they lead you from the first one, by the Carballeira de San Lourenzo in Santiago, all the way to the town of Finisterre. Watch out carefully, however, as in the past the route to Finisterre was partially waymarked in *both* directions (there and back as well). The route is also marked with concrete bollards with both the blue-and-yellow stylised ceramic star familiar from parts of other

Marker stone on the Finisterre route

caminos (and whose rays, not points, indicate the direction you should take). Some of them also indicate the distance remaining to Finisterre, while others give the number of kilometres left to reach Muxia.

Some **maps** are available in Santiago bookshops, such as the 1:250.000 map of Galicia (published by the Xunta de Galicia) and the relevant sheets *(hojas)* of the IGN's 1:25.000 series of the Mapa Topográfico Nacional de España: 94-IV (Santiago), 94-III (Negreira), 94-I (A Baña), 93-II (Mazaricos), 93-I (Brens), 92-II (Corcubión) and 92-IV (Fisterra). For the Finisterre–Muxía section you will need 67-IV (Touriñan) and 67-II (Muxía) *(hojas* 93-1, 93-2 and 92-2).

Accommodation: Apart from the *refugios* mentioned above and the one in Finisterre itself, *hostal/fonda* accommodation is also readily available in Negreira, Cée, Corcubión and Finisterre, as well as the more spartan options of sleeping in the old school in Vilaserio and the sports hall in Cée.

Food: You will pass some shops and bars along the way but it is better to take at least some reserve supplies with you.

Fisterrana: This is a certificate of pilgrimage given by the *Concello* (town hall) in Finisterre to those who have completed the route and have had their *credenciales* (pilgrim passports, from the route they walked prior to Santiago) stamped at intervals along the way. You can make enquiries about this in the *refugio* in Finisterre.

THE ROUTE

From the **Praza do Obradoiro** in Santiago, and with your back to the Cathedral, pass in front of the **Hostal de la Reyes Católicos** (on your R), down the slope in front of its garage (this is the **Costa do Cristo**), go down some steps and along the **Calle de las Huertas** ahead. Veer R at end into **Campo de las Huertas,** continue ahead down **Calle del Cruceiro del Gayo** (the first of two streets in front of you) and then along the **Rúa da Poza de Bar** (unnamed at start); this then becomes the Calle de San Lorenzo.

At the **Carballeira de San Lourenzo** *(a small, shady park with seats, a fountain and a lot of old oak trees)* there is the first yellow arrow. Here you can either:

a) KSO ahead to visit the (former Franciscan monastery) church of **San Lourenzo de Trasouto** *(normal visiting hours Tuesdays and Thursdays 11am–1pm and 4.30–6.30pm, otherwise open at Mass times)* and then retrace your steps, crossing the **Carballeira** diagonally alongside monastery wall and veering L to pick up *camino* ahead, or:

b) turn R immediately (coming from the Cathedral) down the **Roblada de San Lourenzo** (signposted 'Sanatorio'). Shortly afterwards veer L down a cement road **(Corredoira dos Muiños)** leading you downhill to cross bridge over **Río Sarela** in hamlet of…

1km Ponte Sarela

The first house by the bridge has a sign 'Parroquia de San Fructuoso, Lugar de Puente Sarela'; (the old buildings by the bridge were tanneries and the mills used to power them).

From here for the next 7km to Ventosa, in order to avoid the main road, the route is extremely fiddly, with constant changes of direction.

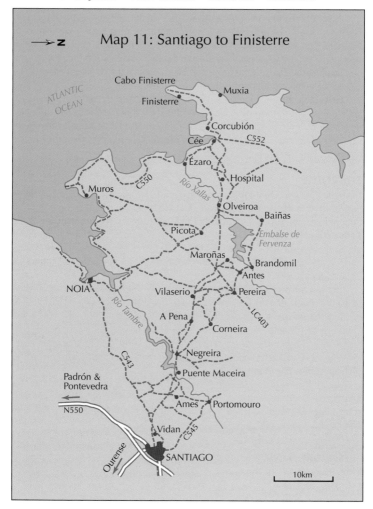

Map 11: Santiago to Finisterre

Cabo Finisterre
Muxia
Finisterre
ATLANTIC OCEAN
Corcubión
C552
Cée
Ézaro
Hospital
Río Xallas
Muros
C550
Olveiroa
Baiñas
Picota
Embalse de Fervenza
Marroñas
Brandomil
Antes
NOIA
Vilaserio
Pereira
LC403
Río Tambre
A Pena
Corneira
Negreira
Padrón & Pontevedra
C543
Puente Maceira
N550
Ames
Portomouro
Vidan
C545
Ourense
SANTIAGO

10km

Turn L on other side of bridge, fork L on bottom of two lanes, gently uphill, and cross stream by small stone FB and stepping stones. KSO(L) at fork shortly afterwards and KSO at crossing and continue on grassy track uphill through meadow.

KSO(R) up FP between hedges (passing to RH side of electric pylon) and join one wider track coming from R then two more, veering L to reach minor road *(2km after Ponte Sarela)*. Turn L downhill and 300m later on turn R up a tarred lane uphill, which continues as a walled lane. KSO(L) at fork. At another junction 400m later, despite *old* arrows to L, turn *right* here. KSO(L) at fork and KSO(R) at next.

KSO(R) on track coming from back L, KSO(R) at fork then turn L downhill at staggered crossing *(all this section is through eucalyptus woods)* and then turn L at crossing at bottom 250m later. Turn R onto minor road 60m later and L 80m later at junction. KSO(R) at turn, turn L at junction 100m later, KSO(L) on unpaved road 100m after that then turn L onto earth track. Veer R to minor road and turn L downhill to road junction by bus shelter and long *hórreo* in…

2km Piñeiro

Turn R. Fork L at fork in hamlet, veering R then L down earth road, following it round to L. Just before you reach a minor road turn R up smaller road uphill which becomes a lane. Turn L 300m later then immediately fork R into woods *(1.5km after Piñeiro)*. KSO, ignoring turns and climbing gradually. At T-junction on level turn L. Reach minor road and turn R then turn L onto track 200m later, passing yellow gas post with '102' on top. After this track becomes a FP for a while, straight ahead downhill, then you join a wider track coming from L and forking R ahead downhill again to road. KSO along it.

Checking the route on the way to Finisterre (Photo: Paddy Dillon)

At junction turn L and immediately R by bus shelter and *cruceiro* down lane, turn L and L again at bottom to T-junction with sports centre on L. Turn R along road and cross...

3.5km Bridge over Río Roxos
Picnic area on other side.

Fork L uphill. Turn R at fork (road becomes an earth track) and then turn R into woods, veering L and then R and turning L at T-junction in **Portela**. After 150m reach a road at entrance (on L) to **Roxos** *(this is the* **Alto do Vento**) and boundary of the *Concello de Ames* (that is, turn L to Santiago). *Bar/mesón opposite.*

Turn R downhill into...

1.5km Ventosa 130m

Turn R by bus shelter and KSO, veering L downhill on old road. Cross road again (by another bus shelter) and KSO on other side under pergolas. Pass between buildings, turn R and then turn R again at front of huge electricity pylon. Turn L onto very minor road then immediately L on a bigger one, then 100m later at junction *(shop on L)* KSO ahead down into...

2km Augapesada 60m
Mesón on R. Medieval bridge (recently restored), picnic area.

Continue downhill to junction. Turn L (signposted 'Bertamirans 3') then turn R up small concrete road uphill *(bar 50m further on, on L after turn)* which becomes a forest track. KSO at crossing *(two handy seats on R)*, continuously uphill.

When you reach a minor road (to L) turn R *(a third seat on R shortly afterwards)*. KSO, passing fourth seat and fifth (on L) just before road (on L). Turn R here and continue on track uphill. Return to road by sixth seat and TV mast and turn R uphill along it. Pass second TV mast and 200m later on R (by sign 'Trasmonte – Santa María') pass fountain. About 200m later begin to go downhill and enter...

2km Carballo 265m

Continue on road, passing wayside cross on wall (R) and KSO at junction in…

1km Trasmonte 220m

Baroque church of Santa María and *cruceiro* (with figure of Santiago) to L. Bar/shop.

Continue on road, passing through **Reino** and **Burgeiros**. KSO on road, turn L at junction and reach…

2km Ponte Maceira 160m

Bar/restaurant. Picturesque village in two parts with stone bridge (five main arches) over the Río Tambre, constructed late 15th/early 16th centuries and restored in medieval style in the 18th century. Capilla de San Blas and large neo-medieval *pazo* on other side of bridge and several stone houses with armorial devices. (Romanesque church of Santa María de Portor 1km to north – tower visible from here.)

Turn R over bridge, turn L uphill at end and 200m later fork L downhill and then turn L down minor road, // to river, veering R.

Continue on track straight ahead, past fields and through woods, then under arch of 19th-century bridge, the **Ponte Maceira Nova** *(bar on other side)* and along riverside, then alongside road (below it to L). Return to road (after 1km) by car dealers in…

2km Barca 150m

KSO on road for 600m, then fork L (signposted 'Logrosa') past industrial buildings, uphill, ignoring turns to R or L. KSO(L) ahead to…

1.5km Chancela 190m

Pass entrance gates (L) to large **Pazo de Chancela** *(also known as Pazo de Capitán – watch out for* **very** *large, loose dogs)* and KSO ahead, ignoring turns, following road down to 'stop' sign. Turn L, pass large statue of pilgrim (L), then pass second statue *(of Minerva and the bulls)* and fountain, veering R uphill **(Avenida de Santiago)**.

🏠 1.5km Negreira 160m

Small town with all facilities, including *hostal* and *fonda. Refugio.*

Turn L (signposted 'Campo de Feria') down the **Carreira de San Mauro** and continue to bottom, passing under archway linking the **Capilla del Carmen y Santa María** on R and the **Pazo de Cotón**, a medieval fortress restored in the 17th century on L. *(Modern statue on R is of the* emigrante/segadora *figure, with a boy pulling at father's trousers through window and mother and child seated.)*

 Cross bridge over **Río Barcala** and at fork turn L uphill and 200m later, at next fork, bear R, marked 'Negreira-Iglesia', then turn R at *cruceiro* to 18th-century church of **San Xulián**. Turn L up steps and R along lane, continuing straight ahead onto tarred lane, on the level. When this bends hard R downhill KSO(L) ahead on RH of two // grassy lanes on L, still on the level, then climbing gently, through eucalyptus woods, with road away to R below. Pass concrete (public services) building on R and KSO, reaching road (CP 56031) 200m later. KSO on road (uphill) for 500m, passing turning to *Cobas* (R) and turn R opposite *shop* and bus shelter in…

2km Zas/Xas 260m

KSO along lane, passing small *ermita* (R), KSO(R) at fork, KSO(L) at next fork and 100m later KSO(R) again. After last house turn L on LH of two grassy walled lanes.

 KSO(L) at junction and KSO when track joins from back L, KSO(R) at fork, then KSO(L) immediately afterwards on track coming from back L; KSO, then 200m later turn L. Reach a main road 100m from road (L) in **Camiño real** *(270m, bar on road)* and turn R along earth lane. About 300m later turn L down walled lane. At junction 300m later KSO ahead then KSO(L) at next. Cross a minor road 150m later and continue ahead on other side on what looks like a FP but is, in fact, a walled lane.

 This is a very old, historic route, completely overgrown and impassable till the late 1990s, becoming wider as you proceed, // to the 'main' road all the time.

 Cross another very minor road and KSO ahead, in a straight line all the time. KSO when track joins from back L, veering R and almost immediately turn L, again in a straight line ahead, // to road. Turn L at crossing 150m later. KSO(R) ahead when track joins from back L, becoming a walled lane leading downhill. KSO(L) ahead when track joins from back R and continue to very minor road in…

4.5km Rapote 330m

Cross over and continue on concrete lane ahead, turn L and then R through village to continue ahead at end down sunken walled lane downhill, ignoring turns, till you reach the bottom. Turn R then KSO(L) uphill on walled lane, ignoring turns till you reach a minor road in...

2km Peña/A Pena 260m

Bar on road (turn L, R and L by first house; simple meals).
Otherwise (to continue): continue ahead, KSO(R) ahead below church and turn L at *cruceiro* uphill, then turn L again to road and turn R. KSO (this is **Porto Camiño**, a pass, 380m) for 400m on road, then just after turning to *Xallas* (on L) turn R onto track and then immediately L ahead (on third from L of the four tracks in front of you) by a concrete water tank. KSO(L) at fork and continue downhill, ignoring turns. Cross stream, veer R and then L uphill again and at a T-junction turn L. Return to road and turn R. About 2km later, just before sharp LH bend, turn L down walled lane into...

4.5km Vilaserio 360m
Bar on R.

Fork (not turn) R downhill behind bar and turn L on road. Pass turning (L) to *Pesadoira* and KSO on road, veering L up to crossroads and turn R into...

2km Cornado

Turn L in village, then 150m later fork L uphill on earth road. At fork KSO(L) ahead till you reach a road (CP5604 KM 18). KSO for 300m then turn L down lane. KSO, ignoring turns, gently uphill.

At top (marker stone 50,266) KSO ahead, gradually downhill, then 150m later fork L at fork uphill. At T-junction 250m after that turn R and fork L at fork after another 250m. *(Shell and 'Maroñas' on one side of marker stone, 'Neria' and shell on other.)* KSO at crossing, KSO at next, cross bridge over river and enter...

4km Maroñas

Shop on road, bar.

Turn L in centre of village, following road round and turn L at end, continuing on lane to T-junction, then turn L at *cruceiro* in centre of…

1km Santa Mariña 330m

12th-century Romanesque church.

Continue to L and turn R along lane to 'main' road. Turn L and continue on road for 500m *(two bars on R: first one may do simple meals)* then turn R uphill (signposted 'Bon Xesús & Guiema'). Continue on road for 3km to two scarcely separated hamlets and turn L in the first one (**Bon Xesús**, 371m). KSO uphill into the second (**Vilar de Xastro**, with simple *cruceiro* on LH side of road) and turn R when you get there, veering L, then fork L up track along RH shoulder of **Monte Aro** (555m), climbing steadily *(good views on a clear day)*. KSO at crossing 100m later, veering L *(views out over reservoirs when track levels out)* and veering R, to junction 500m after that. Turn R then 100m later turn L, downhill, on unpaved road. Continue downhill. Part way down turn *hard* L. Veer R at bottom into…

2km Lago 340m

Turn L and continue out of village on very minor road. About 300m later turn L at T-junction.

Continue on road for 400m and turn R downhill by bus shelter. KSO(R) at junction then KSO(L) ahead at fork. *(Sudden view of line of 20–30 modern windmills on the horizon ahead.)* About 700m later turn R then 250m later turn L. KSO on road till you reach the small church of…

3km San Cristovo de Corzón 286m

Continue on road, past church with separate bell tower, *cruceiro* and cemetery, then 100m later turn L. KSO, ignoring turns. Cross bridge over small river and KSO.

Reach 'main' road in **Mallón** (270m). Cross bridge over **Río Xallas** (and enter *Concello de Dumbría*, leaving the *Concello de Mazaricos*) in…

1.5km Ponte Olveira 270m

KSO(L) at fork 100m after bridge. KSO for 2km, passing *farmacia* (L) and turning to *Santiago Oliveira* (R). KSO and then opposite road KM 22, fork L down minor road into...

🏠 2km Olveiroa 286m

Not to be confused with Olveira, another village nearby. Bar 50m off route to R uphill, *refugio* in centre (with volunteer wardens in the summer months).

Village with several *hórreos* and interesting examples of vernacular architecture. Church of Santiago with statue of St James inside and painted relief sculpture over front door.

KSO through village and 500m later turn L by *lavadero*, crossing small river then, at junction by telephone pylon, *fork* L up small concrete road (near 'main' road) uphill. About 300m later fork R onto an earth road. When you reach telephone cables fork L up another track.

This is a very nice section, apart from the two large, belching carbide factories on the skyline, the first of which is just outside the village of **Hospital***. The camino undulates on a wide track high up, with the mountains all around and the Río Hospital below you to the L.*

Descend fairly rapidly, cross stone FB over river and continue on FP on other side, veering L alongside river, then veering R to a junction with another FP at marker stone 32,066. Turn R uphill to a wider track and turn R. KSO at junction when track joins from back L. Fork R downhill into...

Stone formation near Logoso

3.5km Logoso

KSO(R) and then KSO(L) uphill at end of hamlet and continue on wide, undulating track, high up, across the shoulder of the mountain. Reach the top of the hill and view of carbide factory ahead (L) and turn R onto unpaved road in…

1km Hospital 330m

A village likely, given its name, to have had a pilgrim hospital in the past, though no evidence remains.

Double marker stone where route for Finisterre and Muxia divide

Turn L immediately and L again onto road by KM 27 (P340A) towards the factory. *(Bar on L at top of hill does food.)* Turn R onto old minor road at marker stone 29,353, veering R to 'main' road by factory and 100m later cross it. Here there is a double marker stone and you can either:

a) turn R for direct continuation to *Muxia* (27km, missing out Finisterre; this option is not described here) or:

b) turn L to continue directly to *Finisterre*.

For option b) turn L and KSO on road for 600m then turn R onto track which becomes old walled lane.

This is the old **Camino real**, *the beginning of 9km of drove road leading through the mountains to Cée,* more or less in a straight line, with splendid views on a clear day.

Pass marker stone 27,967 and KSO. KSO(L) at fork 100m later. Cross main road (*cruceiro* in middle) and KSO on other side. Pass marker stone 26,285 and KSO. Veer gradually L and KSO on wide *camino* with open vistas to all sides, 'roof of the world' style. Descend gradually, reach T-junction 1km later and turn R. KSO then turn L downhill 400m after that and 100m later reach…

5.5km Santuario de Nosa Señora das Neves 270m

Small church in shady grounds (nice place for a rest), restored in 1997. The Fonte Santa, a fountain below the road to the L by the *cruceiro*, is well known for its curative properties. A *romería* (local pilgrimage) takes place here annually, on 8 December.

Turn R below church, veering L then R uphill, ignoring turns. Reach marker stone 23,508 and KSO(R) uphill. KSO, KSO(L) at fork. *(Plantations of eucalyptus trees to either side.)* Pass RH turn and 100m later reach junction at marker stone 21,878. Turn L and 50m later KSO(R) at LH turn. About 200m later pass church of…

2.5km San Pedro Mártir 310m

Small chapel set in a field, with its own *fonte santa* (water reputedly cures rheumatism, painful feet and verrucas...), focus of local pilgrimage and another good place for a rest.

Turn R to visit the chapel then retrace your steps.

KSO, ignoring turns. Pass marker stone 19,356, (ignore turning to R) and KSO. *First view of sea ahead and Cape Finisterre, Monte-de-Gozo style, after which you descend, gradually.*

At fork with paved section to R and earth track to L, KSO(L), descending steadily. Veer R, turn L and descend steeply. *(View of another belching factory below, in Cée.)* Reach a minor road at marker stone 16,918 and turn L. Turn *hard* R immediately, downhill, R again at bottom to *cruceiro* and KSO(R), after 'stop' sign, along 'main' road in…

♨ 4.5km Cée 5m

Coastal town with all facilities and several *hostales*.

Church of Nosa Señora de Xunqueira (with Gothic section). In hamlet of **Ameixenda** on coast, 2km to south of Cée, church of Santiago has a relic reputed to be one of the saint's fingers.

Turn R and KSO for 500m, fork L downhill (signposted 'Casa do Concello, Centro de Saude') then turn L, cross street and go down steps/slope to **Rúa Rosalia de Castro**. From there you can:

a) make your way down to waterfront and KSO along it for 1km to Corcubión *(across on other side of bay)* then go up slope*** (L) to main road;

b) to visit town: turn R into **Rúa Rosalia de Castro** and KSO. Cross a square **(Praza da Constitución**, *trees, seats)* from one end to the other then turn L and then R, passing between church (R) and **Casa do Concello** (L). Turn L, crossing grassed area with trees, cross canal and reach waterfront. Continue along it and when road starts to go uphill *** cross over; 200m later fork R up steep concrete street at entrance board for Corcubión. *(However, when the **Paseo maritimo** is completed you will have the further option of continuing along the waterfront here.)*

KSO uphill, KSO(L) at fork (the **Calle Rafael Juan** but not named at start) and then continue along it when it becomes **Calle Antonio Porrúa**, passing the **Capilla del Pilar** (1931) and *fountain* (L) to small square (**Plaza de Castelao**, *seats, trees, taxi rank*) and leave by top LH corner (the **Paseo de San Marcos**) veering L to 13th-century **church of San Marcos** (*large statue of San Roque in pilgrim gear in niche in RH wall*) in…

🏠 1.5km Corcubión 12m
All facilities. Bar Sirena has rooms.

Facing church door turn *hard* R up some steps and up the street ahead (*Calle San Marcos – note houses with armorial devices*) to another square (**Campo de Rollo**). KSO along its LH edge, continue ahead, forking R at first fork and L at second, up **Camino de Vilar**, and follow road as it zigzags uphill. KSO at crossing and then veer L towards main road at top. Cross over and continue on old road on other side (*marker stone 12,468, sports pitch, trees, shady place for a rest*, cruceiro *and fountain on LH side – the* **Fonte de Vilar**). At junction KSO ahead down FP (*this is the* **Encrucijada de San Roque**, main road = C552). Continue along boundary wall (*fountain*) on R, downhill, down grassy lane, descending gradually. Return to road 500m later in hamlet of…

2km Amarela

KSO on road for 400m till it bends sharp L, then cross over and KSO(R) on section of old road. About 80m later turn R down wide grassy lane, reaching road again 100m later near sea. Turn R and KSO on road into…

🏠 1.5km Estorde 50m
Nice beach, campsite (Camping Ruta Finisterre, closed in winter), Hostal Playa de Estorde, bars.

KSO on road for 1km to…

1km Sardiñeiro 20m
Another nice beach; shops, bars.

Just *before* you enter the village watch out for arrows and turn L down lane by block of flats at town entry name board. This short-cuts a bend and then returns to the road. Cross over and fork L down **Rúa do Mestre Barrera** and return to road by *Pensión Nicola* (L). About 200m later, by house no 31, turn R up **Rúa do San Xoan** (signposted to 'Praia do Rostro' and church) then fork L immediately uphill **(Rúa de Fisterra)**. At T-junction 200m after last house turn L along grassy walled lane uphill through eucalyptus woods.

KSO at crossing 600m later and at another, and shortly afterwards emerge with a view out to sea and 'the end of the world' on the second hill ahead of you. Veer R to return to road just past a lay-by with picnic area. Cross over and continue ahead downhill and then up *(steep FP to L midway, leading to quiet secluded beach 50m below you)* and return to road after bend (300m later).

Around 350m after that (at marker stone 6,484) fork L down the **Corredoira de Don Camilo**.

*This is a paved walkway, named after the Nobel prize-winning Galician novelist José Camilo Cela. It runs alongside the sea for 2km, tarmac at first, leading down to and then along the **Praia de Langosteira.** It continues all the way to the entrance of Finisterre (2km), ending at a viewpoint with a cruceiro, and has cafés and chiringuitos (snack bars) at points along it in summer. Or, if you want (and if the tide is suitable) you can walk along the beach itself (sea water good for tired, sore, blistered feet...).*

Sunset over the sea near Finisterre (Photo: Ysabel Halpin)

When you get to the end of the *corredoira* (this area is known as **San Roque**) go up slope to wayside cross and *mirador* (viewpoint) and continue on LH side of the road. KSO down **Calle Santa Catalina**, veering R downhill into centre of town (port to your L).

🏛 4km Finisterre 24m

Small fishing port with all facilities. Modern *refugio* near port. Several *hostales* and *pensiones*.

From the town of Finisterre it is a further 3km to the lighthouse ('el faro') and the real 'end of the earth'.

To walk there: cross street and continue ahead up **Rúa Real** *(refugio on LH corner)* to **Plaza de la Constitución** then straight on down **Calle Plaza to Plaza de Ara Solis**. Turn R and then turn L in front of **Capilla de Nuestra Señora del Buen Suceso** *(note house with armorial device, cross and sundial to R)*. Continue along **Calle Ara Solis**, veering R uphill. Cross **Calle Manuel Lago Paris** and continue uphill to join C552 coming from back R and reach church of…

1km Santa María das Areas

12th-century parish church of 'Saint Mary of the Sands', Romanesque in part, with statue of St James. Gothic *cruceiro*, chapel which was formerly a pilgrim hospital and which had its own Porta Santa in jubilee years. Open 10am–1pm, 3–7pm.

Continue for 2km more on road to the lighthouse.

Fountain – Fonte Cabanas – on R, halfway along). A rocky outcrop known as the 'Piedras Santas', a possible focus of pre-Christian worship, is apparently to be found on the north shore of the peninsula. Hospedaje O Semáforo (in former observatory and morse radio station) with rooms and restaurant, Bar O Refugio. Bronze sculpture of pair of broken boots on rocks behind lighthouse in memory of a pilgrim who drowned here in the late 1990s (this section along the sea is known as the **Costa da Morte** *– 'death coast' – because of the innumerable shipwrecks in times gone by). As the weather is often misty until about midday in this part of Spain you may have better views from here in the late afternoon and evening.*

Return to Santiago by bus (from the long, low building in the port) – three to four journeys a day, Mondays to Saturdays, the last one leaving at at 4pm (6pm on

Atlantic coast near Finisterre (Photo: Paddy Dillon)

The 'end of the earth' beyond the lighthouse on Cape Finisterre (Photo: Ysabel Halpin)

Sundays and holidays). Journey time two to three hours, though the service is not always direct and you may have to change in Vimianzo to connect (immediately) with another bus. Space permitting, it is possible to take one or two bikes. If you want to check return times before you leave Santiago you can ring the bus company (Transportes Finisterre/Arriva) on 981.56.29.24.

APPENDIX A
Camino Aragonés

The *Camino aragonés* was the one taken by those who had crossed the Pyrenees by the Somport Pass after following the Arles route via Montpellier, Toulose and Auch, and joins the *Camino francés* in Puenta la Reina (Navarra: this route also passes through another Puente la Reina in the province of Huesca). There are several *variante* routes in different sections of this *camino,* but only one, waymarked throughout with the familiar yellow arrows, is given here.

It is some 160km from the Somport Pass to Puenta la Reina along the *Camino aragonés* and should take a fairly fit walker six to seven days. It is not a very strenuous route after Jaca and much of the walking is either on the level or downhill, following the valley of the river Aragón as far as Sangüesa. Much of the area is only sparsely inhabited and it is advisable to carry enough water and a certain amount of food. The *Codex Calixtinus* divided the *Camino aragonés* up into three stages, the first beginning in Borce on the French side of the Pyrenees. The second went from Jaca to Monreal and the third from there to Puenta la Reina (Navarra).

Jaca can be easily reached by bus from Zaragoza; **Candanchú** and **Somport** by bus from Jaca. For up-to-date information regarding accommodation on this route it is advisable to consult the Confraternity of St James's guide to the Arles route.

Somport

5km Canfranc estación
Tourist office, shops, bars, restaurant,
Albergue Pepito Grillo, hotel

4km Canfranc pueblo
Albergue Sargantan

5km Villanúa
Shops, bars, restaurants, Albergue
Tritón

7km Castiello de Jaca
Supermarket, mesón (rooms)

8.5km Jaca
All facilities, refugio

15km Santa Cilia
Shop, bar

6km Puenta la Reina
Hotel/restaurant, hostal/restaurant

16km Mianos

4.5km Artieda
Shop

10.5km Ruesta

23km Undués de Lerda
Bar (meals), refugio

10.5km Sangüesa
All facilities, refugio

5km Liédena
Shop, hostal/restaurant

6km Lumbier
Shop, mesón

4.5km Nardués

1km Aldunate

5km Izco
Refugio

2km Abinzano

2km Idocín

5km Salinas

2km Monreal
Shop, hostal/restaurant

4km Yárnoz

1.5km Otano

2km Esperun

1.5km Guerendiáin

3.5km Tiebas
Shop, bar, refugio

1km Campanas
Restaurant

3km Biurrun

3.5km Ucar

2km Enériz
Shop, mesón

2km Eunate

6km Puenta la Reina
All facilities, two refugios

APPENDIX B
Summary of St James's and other Pilgrim References

Valcarlos
- Church of Santiago contains life-size representation of *Santiago Matamoros*

Roncesvalles
- Chapel of Santiago with modern statue of St James above the altar

Alto de Erro
- Venta del Caminante/Venta del Puerto, a former pilgrim inn

Larrasoaña
- Church contains statue of St James
- Former pilgrim hospital

Zabaldica
- Church contains statue of St James

Trinidad de Arre
- Basilica had small pilgrim hospital in former times

Pamplona
- Puente de los Peregrinos, old bridge over the Arga, with recently decapitated statue of St James on small column at far end
- Cathedral has stained-glass St James in window of apostles, Capilla Barbanara, east cloister gallery
- Church of Santo Domingo was formerly church of Santiago: i) main façade with statue of *Santiago Apóstol* above main portal; ii) statue of *Santiago Peregrino* in retable above main altar
- Church of San Cernin/San Saturnino has *Santiago Peregrino* with scrip with scallop on it and tiny pilgrim kneeling at his feet, main façade
- Church of San Nicolás, south wall, retable of San Miguel, has St James with 'bleeding heart', scallops and staff
- Diocesan Museum, Cathedral: i) polychrome wood statue of *Santiago Apóstol* rom Artajona (near Puente la Reina); ii) polychrome wood statue of San Roque from Ayegui (on *camino* after Estella)
- Former pilgrim hospitals in Calle Dormitaleria 13, Calle Compania 3 and in the building that is now the Museo de Navarra
- Bronze plaque (modern) with scallop shells and representations of Milky Way in front of Santo Domingo in Plaza de Santiago

Cizor Menor
- Remains of old pilgrim hospital

Gambellacos
- Fuente de Reniega (modern), recalling the legend of the pilgrim tempted by the devil to renounce the church and St James but saved by the saint disguisd as a pilgrim who led him to this hidden fountain

Monte del Perdón

- Modern bronze statues of pilgrims, mounted pilgrims and dog erected by Navarre Association

Muruzábal

- Statue of *Santiago Peregrino* inside church of San Estéban

Puente la Reina

- Church of Santiago with statue of *Santiago Peregrino* inside
- Modern statue of pilgrim at junction of routes (at entrance to town)

Estella

- Church of San Sepulcro: i) St James in frieze above north portal; ii) statue of St James at side of north portal

Ayegui

- Former pilgrim hospice attached to the monastery

Irache

- Pilgrim statue (modern bas-relief) above wine fountain operated by Bodegas Irache

Villamayor de Monjardín

- Modern St James bas-relief on wall of house

Viana

- Church of Santa María: i) polychrome statue of *Santiago Peregrino* on RH side of altarpiece; ii) altarpiece in east end, NE chapel has a) *Santiago Matamoros* on top

and b) panel of the Virgen del Pilar appearing to St James
- Tiny pilgrim in niche on house on corner of Calle la Rueda

Logroño

- Cathedral of Santa María Redonda has i) carving of St James in choir stalls; ii) polychrome statue of San Roque in chapel on north wall
- Church of Santiago with i) massive equestrian statue of *Santiago Matamoros* above south door; ii) polychrome statue of *Santiago Peregrino* on main altarpiece
- Church of San Bartolomé has lintel of apostles, with St James third from L, tympanum of main portal
- Museo de la Rioja has i) pair of paintings, left St John and St James, right St James among the disciples, from Ribalmaguillo; ii) polychrome wood statue of *Santiago Peregrino* from main altarpiece of San Jeronimo del Monasterio de la Estrella in San Ascenio (near Logroño); iii) polychrome wood statue of San Roque
- Modern pavement board game of pilgrim churches, bridges, etc, outside church of Santiago, Plaza de Santiago

Navarrete

- Gates from 12th-century pilgrim hospital installed at the entrance to the cemetery when this was established in 1875. On *back* of gate there is a carving of one weathered pilgrim with scrip and staff being force fed by another, RH side

• Church of Asunción de Santa María has polychrome statue of St James, top left, *retablo mayor*

Alto de San Antón
• Ruins of convent with pilgrim hospital

Azófra
• Church of Nuestra Señora de los Angeles has sculpture of *Santiago Peregrino*, with staff, cape and hat
• Fuente de los Romeros just outside village, near site of 12th-century pilgrim hospital with adjoining cemetery

Santo Domingo de la Calzada
• Cathedral (inside) has i) tiny pilgrim with staffs carved on base of tomb of Santo Domingo inside cathedral; ii) carving of St James to R on west end high choir stalls; iii) St James on LH side altarpiece in Capilla del Retablo (Damien Forment) moved to north wall of cathedral as part of recent restoration
• Cloister of cathedral has i) statue of San Roque, NE corner; ii) *Santiago Apóstol*, south cloister gallery; iii) *Santiago Apóstol*, west cloister gallery
• Pilgrim monument (modern) outside Convento de San Francisco on way out of Santo Domingo

San Millán de Cogilla
• Niche statue of San Roque above main portal
• Ermita de San Roque in village

Clavijo
• Tiny Matamoros – St James on toy horse, parish church interior, next to sword of Santiago

Belorado
• 16th-century church of Santa María: i) Santiago chapel, with retable of life of Santiago; ii) statue of *Santiago Matamoros* above *Santiago Peregrino*

Villambistia
• Chapel of San Roque

Villafranca Montes de Oca
• 18th-century parish church of Santiago with St James statue
• Remains of Hospital San Antonio

Ermita de Valdefuentes
(4km before San Juan de Ortega)
• All that remains of a former pilgrim hospital

San Juan de Ortega
• Base of the catafalque has carving of line of tiny pilgrims receiving bread

Gamonal (suburb of Burgos)
• Stone *crucero* in front of church has *Santiago Peregrino* carved on the shaft – collar of apostles

Cartuja de Miraflores
• Main altarpiece has: i) polychrome statue of St James with staff and boat (top centre right); ii) (bottom left) polychrome statue of Juan II accompanied by St James; iii) (bottom centre left) resting pilgrim with

staff; iv) (bottom centre left) Last Supper – St James to Christ's left, polychrome bas-relief
- Tomb of Juan II and Isabel of Portugal has tiny statue of St James among apostles

Burgos
- Cathedral: i) chapel of Santiago with equestrian satue of St James in upper part of entrance *grille* and in altarpiece; ii) statue of *Santiago Peregrino* with staff and scallop-covered scrip in cloister, east walk; iii) St James among apostles, north Portal de la Coronería, RH side; iv) pilgrim head on cloister capital; v) choirstall carving of the Virgen del Pilar appearing to St James; vi) Capilla de Santa Tecla – equestrian St James; vii) museum: representation of St James
- Church of San Lesmes has bas-relief of St James on altarpiece of the passion, south aisle
- Ermita de San Amaro Peregrino i) statue of *Santiago Peregrino* in niche above main entrance gate; ii) polychrome statue of *Santiago Peregrino* above altar
- Hospital del Rey: i) seated St James in niche above main gate; ii) bas-relief of *Santiago Matamoros* on west tower above Puerta de Romeros; iii) carved wooden doors of Puerta de Romeros with images of *Santiago Peregrino* and pilgrim family and friends
- Monastery of Las Huelgas contains chapel of Santiago and articulated

seated statue of St James used for knighting kings – this is now at the entrance

Hontanas
- Modern plaque with Jacobean decoration – pilgrim, scallops and so on, on house on RH side of *camino* on leaving village

Castrojeriz
- Church of Nuestra Señora del Manzano contains statue of Santiago
- Bas-relief *Santiago Matamoros* on monument halfway along Calle Real

Boadilla
- Scallop-covered *rollo*

Itero de la Vega
- 13th-century Ermita de la Piedad contains statue of *Santiago Peregrino*

Fromista
- Wooden statue of St James in church of St Martín

Población de Campos
- Remains of former pilgrim hospital

Villavieco
(between Fromista and Villasirga)
- Church of Santa María has altarpiece of St James

Villálcazar de Sirga
- 13th-century church of Santa María la Blanca contains: i) chapel of Santiago; ii) a statue of St James on

the altarpiece of the chapel of the north wall which depicts scenes from his life and ministry; iii) alabaster (modern) statue of St James next to tomb of Doña Leonor III in Capilla de Santiago
- Ermita de la Virgen del Río: alabaster statue of *Santiago Peregrino* inside

Carrión de los Condes
- Santiago church (only portal remains, after building was destroyed by fire in AD809 War of Independence). Museum of religious art inside with modern painting of *Santiago Peregrino* by a nun from Palencia
- Real Monasterio de San Zoilo has bas-relief of St James with gourd and staff, east cloister gallery

Santa María de las Tiendas
- Remains of 11th-century pilgrim hospital belonging to the Order of the Knights of Santiago

Ledigos
- Church of Santiago with three different statues of St James

Sahagún
- Church of La Peregrina
- Church of San Lorenzo has polychrome San Roque inside
- Virgen Peregina in museum of the Madres Benedictinas
- Modern St James statue outside Iglesia de la Trinidad (now a *refugio*)

Calzada del Coto
- Ermita de San Roque

Mansilla de las Mulas
- Modern statue of very weary pilgrim at base of *crucero* at entrance to town

León
- Cathedral Santa María de la Regla has: i) St James with panel of Apostles, central portal of north façade ii) St James pilgrim, stained-glass window of the apse; iii) statues of San Roque and Santiago Peregrino in Capilla de Santiago, chapel of north-east ambulatory; iv) statue of *Santiago Peregrino*, left side of Puerta de la Virgen del Dado, north portal of cathedral, adjacent to cloister; v) statue of *Santiago Peregrino*, south portal of cloister; vi) tympanum of Christ Pantocrator with kneeling pilgrims to the right, adjacent to the Puerta de la Gomia, south-west corner of the cloister; vii) tympanum of the Crucifixion, with kneeling pilgrim to the right, adjacent to the Puerta de la Gomia, south-west corner of the cloister; viii) group of pilgrims in one of the Nicolás Francés frescoes, cloister; ix) stained-glass window of Santiago in Capilla de Santiago
- San Marcos, former pilgrim hospital, is now a *parador*
- Church of Convento de San Marcos: i) scallop-shell façade; ii) painting of *Santiago Matamoros* on main altarpiece; iii) polychrome stone statue of *Santiago Peregrino*, north wall of Capilla Mayor
- Convento de San Marcos: i) bas-relief of *Santiago Matamoros* above

the main portal; ii) heads in roundels with hats with scallop shells – several on main façade; iii) several roundels enclosing swords of Santiago on main façade – and bas-reliefs of swords

- Double sacristy in Convento de San Marcos (now a museum): i) bas-relief of *Santiago Matamoros* above the main altar in the first room; ii) stone statue of Santiago in the first room; iii) Flemish wood statue of Santiago Apóstol (from either León cathedral or San Miguel del Camino) in the first room; iv) a painting of Santiago with San Juan Evangelista, in the second room
- Vestibule of the Palacio de los Guzmanes has bas-relief of San Agustín washing the feet of Christ dressed as a pilgrim
- Plaza de San Marcos, modern sculpture of pilgrim with sandals at base of *crucero* opposite church of the Convento de San Marcos

Virgen del Camino

- Large bronze statue of St James pointing the way to Santiago on façade of modern church of San Froilan

Villadangos del Páramo

- Church of Santiago: i) painting of Santiago Matamoros on main west portal, outside; ii) statue of Santiago Matamoros on LH side of main altarpiece, beneath statue of *Santiago Peregrino*

Villar de Mazarife

- Modern mosaic of pilgrims arriving at the church of Villar de Mazarife at entrance to village

Hospital de Orbigo

- Church of San Juan Bautista: i) niche statue, wooden, of *Santiago Peregrino* seated above south portal in the porch; ii) statue of *San Roque Peregrino* on retablo on north wall

Astorga

- Contained 22 pilgrim hospitals in the Middle Ages, the last of which, the Hospital de las Cinco Llagas (the Five Wounds), burned down early in the 20th century
- Cathedral: i) tiny statue of *Santiago Peregrino* above main west portal; ii) bas-relief of procession of pilgrims, tympanum of west portal; iii) statue of Santiago, chapel of north wall; iv) painting of Santiago among other apostles on the side of a wooden chest from the Cistercian monastery of Carrizo de la Ribera, in the diocesan museum
- Museo de los Caminos, Palacio Episcopal has several stone/polychrome wood statues of Santiago
- Church of San Pedro, main façade covered in pilgrim themes: mosaics – route, churches, hospitals and pilgrims – prepared for *Las Edades de del Hombre* (exhibition) in 2000

El Ganso

- Church of Santiago, with chapel of Cristo de los Peregrinos

Rabanal del Camino

- Ermita del Bendito Cristo has statue of San Roque (from former church in Manjarín)
- Church of San José has statue of *Santiago Peregrino*, top of main altarpiece
- Church of Santa María has statue of *Santiago Peregrino* (in vestry)
- Refugio Gaucelmo has modern niche statue of *Santiago Peregrino* above main façade

Foncebadón

- Remains of 11th-century *alberguería*

Cruz de Ferro

- Modern Ermita de Santiago (built for the 1982 Holy Year)

Manjarín

- Remains of former church of San Roque

El Acebo

- Statue of Santiago Peregrino in church of San Miguel

Molinaseca

- Ermita de San Roque (now a *refugio*)
- Church of San Nicolás de Bari has statue of Santiago inside

Ponferrada

- Basilica of Nuestra Señora de la Encina has statue of *San Roque Peregrino*, altar of north transept
- Santa María de Vizbayo de Otero has statue of *San Roque Peregrino* on north side of apse inside

Compostilla

- Modern *crucero* with statue of *Santiago Peregrino* in village

Columbrianos

- Modern painting of *Santiago Peregrino* on outside of Ermita de San Juan
- Modern *crucero* with statue of Santiago Peregrino

Cacabelos

- Town formerly had five pilgrim hospitals of which the San Lázaro is now a restaurant
- Capilla de San Roque

Villafranca del Bierzo

- Church of Santiago with north *puerta del perdón* and statue of *Santiago Peregrino* inside, south wall
- Church of San Francisco has statue of Santiago with flag of the Order of Santiago on the tomb of a servant of Pedro Alvarez de Osorio de Toledo, a member of the order, north wall of the nave
- Santa María del Cluniaco has statue of *San Roque Peregrino*, north wall, west corner of church, inside
- Modern statue of *Santiago Peregrino* adorned with sword of Santiago on Cuesta Zamora (a street) near the Río Burbia (may be a pilgrim??)

Herrerías

- Last houses in village known as Hospital Inglés, with chapel where pilgrims who died en route were buried

O Cebreiro

- Bas-relief of *Santiago Peregrino* on the shaft of the Crucero de Peregrino, entry to village, behind church
- Modern statue of *Santiago Peregrino* outside shop opposite Hospedería San Giraldo de Aurillac

Alto de San Roque

- Chapel of San Roque
- Huge modern statue of *Santiago Peregrino* 'on the move' at side of road

Hospital da Condesa

- Church of Santiago with sword of Santiago on top of tower

Triacastela

- Church of Santiago with i) niche statue of *Santiago Peregrino*, modern, on west tower above west portal; ii) statue of *Santiago Peregrino* on altar mayor
- Antiguo Hospital de Peregrinos, Casa Pedreira, Rúa do Peregrino (main street), RH side, towards bottom
- Modern pilgrim statue at end of town with *Santiago Peregrino* on pyramid with sword of Santiago on pyramid face

Renche

- *Santiago Peregrino* on the retablo mayor of church

Zoo

- Church of Santiago

Furela

- Capilla San Roque

Sarria

- Niche statue of *Santiago Peregrino* (behind bars), LH side, Rúa da Mercade, just before Mosteiro da Magdalena on way out of town on *camino* (in old prison building)
- Hospital de San Antonio, Rúa Maior (now law courts)
- Capilla de San Lázaro has wooden bas-relief of *Santiago Peregrino*, left, and San Roque, right – a modern pair, on the wooden west portal
- Church of Santa Marina, Rúa Maior has painting (modern) of procession of pilgrims going to Santiago on churchyard wall
- Modern wood carving of Santiago Beltza (Santiago Puente la Reina) on a scroll above an arts and crafts shop in Rúa Maior
- Modern carved stèle of a pilgrim to Santiago inside vestibule of Mosteiro da Magdalena

Barbadelo

- Church of Santiago

Marzán O Real

- Modern pilgrim fountain adorned by large 'peregrin' logo

Eirexe/Airexe

- Statue of *Santiago Peregrino* inside church

Lestedo

- Church of Santiago

Palas do Rei

- Modern statue of *Santiago Peregrino*, Travesia del Peregrino

Furelos

- Statue of *San Roque Peregrino*, north wall of church of San Xoán Bautista

Melide

- Church of San Pedro has statue of *San Roque Peregrino* on altar mayor
- Parish church of Sancti Spiritus has painting of *Santiago Peregrino*, north wall
- Church of San Antonio has statue of *Santiago Peregrino* kneeling before the Virgen del Pilar (with child), north wall
- Church of Santa María has *Santiago Apóstol* in left side, apse wall paintings

Boente

- Church of Santiago with statues of *Santiago Peregrino*, *Santiago Matamoros* and *San Roque*, all inside

Ribadaixo

- Former pilgrim hospital in building by river is now pilgrim refuge

Arzúa

- Santiago statue above altar in church of Santa María
- Fountain beside Capela de Magdalena – very weathered bas-relief of *Santiago Peregrino* – head and shoulders with staff and scrip on slab above fountain basin

Lavacolla

- Capilla San Roque

Santiago de Compostela

- **Cathedral:**

i) statue of St James and his companions Anastasius and Theodore above the Puerta Santa

ii) Platerías façade – spindly Santiago Apóstol is to Christ's R in the Apostles frieze above the portal

iii) Azabachería façade – *Santiago Peregrino* flanked by kneeling figures of Alfonso VI and Ordono II at the very top of the facade above the doors

iv) Obradoiro façade: a) centre top *Santiago Peregrino*; b) above entrance to crypt – tiny bas-relief of *Santiago Matamoros*

v) Pórtico de la Gloria: a) St James seated with tau cross on the trumeau and scroll; b) *Santiago Apóstol*, right panel of Apostles

vi) *Santiago Matamoros*: a) west side of north Azabachería arm of the transept – statue in glass case; b) Clavijo tympanum – stone bas-relief of *Santiago Matamoros*, west side of the south, Platerías arm of the transept

vii) Polychrome statue of *Santiago Peregrino*, altarpiece of Capilla de San Bartolomé, northeast ambulatory

viii) Capilla de las Reliquias, south aisle has: a) gilded statuette of Santiago Coquatriz; b) gilded statue of *Santiago Peregrino* of Don Alvaro de Isorno; c) *Santiago Peregrino* – tiny silver statue

ix) Niche statue of *Santiago Peregrino*, west wall of the south (Platerías) arm of the transept above the door to the Sacristy

x) Stained-glass seated *Santiago Peregrino* in the ambulatory above the Holy Door (the inside one)

xi) Chancel – Capilla Mayor has: a) *Santiago Matamoros* crowning the baldechín; b) *Santiago Peregrino* standing on top of the Camerín; c) seated *Santiago Peregrino* in the camarín – the 'hug' Santiago

xii) Neo-Romanesque silver casket containing the body of St James and his disciples Anastasius and Theodore in the crypt under the Capilla Mayor

xiii) Cloister: *Santiago Peregrino*, left side of the altarpiece of the Transfiguration of Christ, Capilla de Alba, northwest corner of cloister

xiv) Polychrome statue of *Santiago Peregrino*, left side of altarpiece of Capilla del Salvador (chapel of the Kings of France), axial chapel of ambulatory

xv) Museum of the Cathedral: a) seated stone polychrome Santiago with tau cross and crown; b) bronze relief of the Translation of the body of the Apostle to Galicia; c) polychrome wood and alabaster retablo of the Life of St James donated by John Goodyear – the Calling, Martyrdom and Translation; d) gilded wood panel of Queen Lupa's stubborn oxen and the apostle's body in the cart in Galicia; e) gilded wood reredos of pilgrims climbing the hill to Santiago; f) gilded wood panel of Moors returning the bells from Córdoba to Santiago; g) polychrome wood relief of Santiago preaching in Galicia

• Colegio de San Geronimo – north portal, statue of *Santiago Peregrino*, left side

• Palacio de Rajoy: *Santiago Matamoros* crowning a triangular pediment of bas-relief of *Santiago Matamoros* at the Battle of Clavijo – main façade

• Hostal de los Reyes Católicos: i) statue of *Santiago Peregrino*, top left upper frieze above the main south portal; ii) statue of *Santiago Peregrino* – centre of the lower frieze of the Apostles above the main south portal; iii) statue of St James, right jamb of main south portal

• Monasterio de San Martín Pinario (in its museum): i) statue of the Virgen del Pilar and Child appearing to a kneeling *Santiago Apóstol*; ii) statue of *Santiago Matamoros*

• Colegiata de Santa María del Sar: i) statue of *San Roque Peregrino* in vestry; ii) statue of *San Roque Peregrino* in north apse

• Pilgrimage museum: i) wood relief, *San Roque Peregrino*; ii) wood statue of a pilgrim; iii) polychrome wood panel painting of Christ as a pilgrim; iv) polychrome wood statue, *San Roque Peregrino*, back of a chest; v) Santa Isabel, 'Reina de Portugal Aragonesa' – dressed as a lady pilgrim; vi) polychrome *Santiago Peregrino* – eight wood ones; vii) polychrome granite

Santiago Peregrino; viii) polychrome wood *Virgen peregrino* with child; ix) stone statue *Santiago Peregrino* three stone ones; x) tapestry/embroidery of *Santiago Apóstol*

- Statue of St James above a fountain near Santo Domingo de Bonneval
- Colegio de Santiago Alfeo/de Fonseca – statue of *Santiago Peregrino* above main portal
- Huge modern statue of *Santiago Peregrino* in middle of roundabout outisde the Xunta de Galica headquarters in the San Caetano area of Santiago (near bus station)

Trasmonte
- Figure of St James on *cruceiro* outside church

Olveiroa
- Church of Santiago with painted bas-relief of saint above church door and statue of St James on main altar

Hospital
- Village with former pilgrim hospital

Cée
- Town formerly had pilgrim hospital

Ameixenda (2km south of Cée)
- Church of Santiago and relic reputed to be one of the saint's fingers

Corcubión
- Town formerly had pilgrim hospital
- Church of San Marcos has large statue of San Roque in pilgrim gear

- Alto de San Roque at top of hill on leaving town

Finisterre
- San Roque area at entry to town
- Statue of St James in church of Santa María das Areas, with cemetery chapel that formerly belonged to its pilgrim hospital

APPENDIX C
Suggestions for Further Reading

General

Atwood, Donald and John, C.R.
Penguin Dictionary of Saints
3rd ed (Harmondsworth: Penguin, 1995)

Charpentier, Louis.
Les Jacques et le mystère de Compostelle
(Paris: Ed Laffont, 1971)

Discusses arguments for the existence of a pre-Christian, possibly pre-Celtic, path to 'land's end' on the Atlantic coast (similar to those through southern Britain to Cornwall and across northern France to Brittany), an initiatory route following the 'Way of the Stars' on which the course of the *Camino francés* is largely based.

Chaucer, Geoffrey.
Canterbury Tales, trans. Nevill Coghill
(London: Penguin Classics, 1977)

Coleman, Simon and Elsner, John.
Pilgrimage past and present in the world's religions
(London: British Museum Press, 1995)

Davies, J.G.
Pilgrimage yesterday and today: why? where? how?
(London: SCM Press, 1988)

Studies the nature of pilgrimages and motives behind them from patristic times to the Middle Ages, Protestant condemnation of pilgrimages and the 19th-century revival of pilgrimages amongst Protestants, ending with a review of the devotional aspects of modern pilgrmages.

Eade, John and Sallnow, Michael J., ed.
Contesting the sacred: the anthropology of Christian pilgrimage
(London: Routledge, 1991)

Contributors examine particular Christian shrines (in France, Italy, Israel, Sri Lanka and Peru), analysing the dynamics of religious expression and belief but also the political and economic processes at local and global levels, emphasising that pilgrimage is primarily an arena for competing religious and secular discourses.

French, R.M. (trans.)
The Way of a Pilgrim
(London: Triangle, 1995)

First published in English in 1930, this book was written by an unknown Russian pilgrim in the 19th century, and tells the story of his wanderings from one holy place to another in Russia and Siberia in search of the way of prayer.

Gitlitz, David M. and Davidson, Linda Kay.
The Pilgrimage Road to Santiago: the complete cultural handbook

(New York: St Martins Press, 2000)

As its title suggests this book provides historical, architectural and cultural information about the places along the route, interspersed with the personal experiences of the authors along the *camino*.

Robinson, Martin.
Sacred places, pilgrim paths: an anthology of pilgrimage
(London: Fount, 1997)

An anthology reflecting the experiences of pilgrims through the ages, dealing with places of pilgrimage, preparation for the journey, the journey itself, the inner journey, worship on the way and on arrival and the questions raised once the pilgrimage is over.

Way of St James

Barret, Pierre and Gurgand, Jean-Noël.
Priez pour nous à Compostelle
(Paris: Hachette, 1978)

An account of the authors' journey from Vézelay to Santiago on foot, interspersed with parallel accounts of pilgrims from previous centuries. Contains a very extensive bibliography.

Bourdarias, Jean and Wasielewski, Michel.
Guide Européen des Chemins de Compostelle
(Paris: Fayard, 1997)

Guide to all the European routes to Santiago (from Holland, Denmark, Poland, Hungary, Brenner, Croatia, Italy and Portugal), not only the currently more well-known routes through France and Spain. Contains maps, distances, over 800 photographs, history and descriptions of places, lives of saints and relevant Biblical extracts.

Burgess, G. (trans.)
Song of Roland
(Penguin Classics, 1990)

Dennett, Laurie.
A hug for the apostle. On foot from Chartres to Santiago de Compostela
(Toronto: Macmillan of Canada, 1987)

An account of the author's walk, undertaken to raise money for the Multiple Sclerosis Society. Some of the book covers the pilgrimage in France, though much of it is devoted to the route in Spain, including much interesting historical material.

Frey, Nancy Louise.
Pilgrim stories
(Berkley & Los Angeles: University of California Press, 1998)

This refers specifically to the experiences of modern pilgrims along the road to Santiago de Compostela, before, during and after making their pilgrimage, but the questions raised confront any modern pilgrim on a route where the journey itself, rather than the destination, is the real issue.

Hogarth, James (trans. from Latin).
The Pilgrim's Guide: a 12th century Guide for the Pilgrim to St. James of Compostela
(Confraternity of St James, 1992)

Jacobs, Michael.
The Road to Santiago de Compostela (Architectural Guides for Travellers series)
(London: Viking, 1990)

A guide to the churches, monasteries, hostels and hospitals along the pilgrim route, analysing their architectural styles. Contains photos, maps and detailed plans.

Laffi, Domenico (trans. James Hall).
A Journey to the West
(Leiden: Primavera Pers/
Santiago: Xunta de Galicia, 1997)

A translation of and commentary on the diary of a 17th-century pilgrim from Bologna to Santiago. Includes maps and 84 original black-and-white illustrations.

Mullins, Edward.
The Pilgrimage to Santiago
(London: Sigma Books, 2001)

An account of the art, architecture, history and geography of the pilgrim route from Paris to Santiago.

Shaver-Crandell, Annie
and Gerson, Paula.
The Pilgrim's Guide to Santiago de Compostela: a Gazeteer
(London/ Langhorne:
Harvey Miller, 1995)

730 entries and 575 illustrations describing all the relics of saints, important monuments, towns and buildings encountered by the 12th-century pilgrim along the four routes through France and then in Spain. Includes a new translation of the Latin text of the *Codex Calixtinus* plus discussion of the pilgrimage phenomenon in the Middle Ages as well as the tradition of travel literature.

Slader, Bert.
Pilgrim Footsteps
(Newcastle, County Down: Quest Books [NI], 1994)

Starkie, Walter.
The Road to Santiago. Pilgrim of St James
(London: John Murray, 1957)

An account of a pilgrimage to Santiago, part travel, part history, part autobiography.

Tate, Brian and Marcus.
The Pilgrim Route to Santiago
(Oxford: Phaidon, 1987)

Explains the pilgrim phenomenon and the history of the shrine as well as discussing the different routes. Contains 137 photographic illustrations by Pablo Keller, 50 of them in colour.

Viellard, Jeanne.
Guide du Pèlerin de Saint Jacques de Compostelle
(Paris: Klincksieck, 4th ed 1989)

A French translation, on facing pages, of what is probably the first known guidebook: Aymery Picaud's 12th-century description of the pilgrim routes to Santiago.

Peregrino magazine

Six issues a year, articles (general, historical, practical, as well as accounts of journeys) on the pilgrimage.

APPENDIX D
Useful Addresses

Confraternity of Saint James
27 Blackfriars Road
London SE1 8NY

Tel: (020) 7928 9988

Email: office@csj.org.uk
www.csj.org.uk

on-line bookshop:
www.csj.org.uk/ bookshop

Stanfords
12 Long Acre
Covent Garden
London WC2E 9LP

Tel:(020) 7836 1321

www.stanfords.co.uk

The Map Shop
15 High Street
Upton-upon-Severn
Worcs WR8 0HJ

Tel: (01684) 593146

www.themapshop.co.uk

Peregrino, Boletin
del Camino de Santiago
Apartado 60
26250 Santo Domingo de la Calzada
La Rioja
Spain

Bookshops in Santiago
Librería Egeria
Plaza de la Inmaculada 5
Upmarket religious bookshop

Librería San Pablo
Rúa do Vilar 39
Religious/general bookshop

Librería Encontros
Rúa do Vilar 68
Religious/general bookshop

Librería Gali
Rúa do Vilar 66
General bookshop

Follas Novas
Montero Ríos 37
University/general bookshop

Abraxos Libros
Montero Ríos 50
Univeristy/general bookshop

APPENDIX E
Glossary

agua (non) potable	(not) drinking water
agua non tratada	'untreated' (chlorine-free) water
albergue	inn; also used to refer to a *refugio* (pilgrim hostel)
alcalde	mayor
alcázar	fortress, castle
aldea	hamlet
almacén	warehouse, store
alto	hill, height
andadero	paved/surfaced walkway, often at side of main road (similar to a cycle track)
arcén	hard shoulder, verge
arroyo	stream, small river
ayuntamiento	town hall
barrio	suburb
bascula	weighbridge
bodega	wine cellar; also used to describe a storage place for wine located in hillsides and other places in the open countryside
cafetería	a café that also serves snacks (not a self-service restaurant for hot meals)
calzada	(paved) road, causeway
camino	track, path
camino de sirga	towpath
cancela	outer door/gate; wrought-iron/lattice gate
capilla	chapel
carretera	(main) road, highway
Casa Consistorial	town hall in small places
Casa do Concello	town hall (in Galicia)
casa huéspedes (CH)	guest house
casco antiguo	historic quarter (of a town)
cierren la puerta/el portillo	'close the gate'
cigüena	stork

circunvalación	by-pass, ring road
colegiata/colexiata	collegiate church
coto de caza	hunting/game preserve
coto de pesca	fishing preserve
crucero	wayside cross
¡cuidad con el perro!	beware of the dog
dehesa	estate; pastureland
depósito de agua	water tower
desvío	detour, diversion (for example, on roads)
embalse	dam, reservoir
encina	holm oak (an evergreen variety)
ermita	originally a hermitage but nowadays frequently used to describe a small church or chapel
estanco	kiosk (selling tobacco, stamps, and so on)
estrada	main road, highway (Galicia)
finca	small holding
fonda	guest house, inn
frontón	pelota court
fuente	fountain, spring
gallego	Galician
gasolinera	petrol station
'la general'	'main road' (= *carretera general*)
hórreo	(raised) granary
hospedaje	a *fonda* (in Galicia)
hospedería	inn, hostelry
hostal	hotel (less expensive than a *hotel*)
igrexia/eirexa	church (Galician)
ixti ataka mesedez	'close the gate' (Basque)
jacobeo	(adj) of St James
jara	cistus (bush)
lavadero	outdoor washing place, (public) wash-house

merendero	picnic area, refreshment stall
meseta	plateau, tableland
mesón	restaurant (often simple, with period/regional decor)
mosteiro	monastery (Gallego)
nave	nave (in church); hangar; industrial building
palloza	round thatched dwelling of Celtic origin
palmero	pilgrim who has been to Jerusalem
panadería	bakery
pantano	marsh, swamp (natural); reservoir, dam (artificial)
páramo	plain, bleak plateau (often used in place names)
paseo	stroll, walk; avenue
paso canadiense	cattle grid
peregrino	pilgrim
plaza de toros	bull ring
posada	inn (simpler than a fonda)
pueblo	village, small town
puente	bridge
puerta	door, gateway
puerto	mountain pass; port
repetidor	TV/radio masts, transmitter, antenna
rollo	stone wayside cross, often at junctions; raised up and may be highly decorated
rodeo	roundabout or indirect route
romería	pilgrimage to a local shrine
romero	pilgrim (originally one who had been to Rome)
rúa	street (Galician)
santuario	church where, originally, relics of a saint were believed to be kept
sellar	to (rubber) stamp
sello	stamp, seal
senda	(small) path, track
señal	waymark, signal
tapas	light snack taken with drinks in a bar
travesía	cross-street, short street which joins two others

ultramarinos	grocer's shop
vega	fertile plain, lowland area, valley (often found in place names)
venta/venda	country inn (in former times)
villa	small town

One or two **linguistic hints** may help to equate the Galician words to the Castilian ('Spanish') ones you probably already know (Galician is sometimes described as 'Portuguese with Castilian spelling'). For example:

- dropping intervocalic consonants
  (for example, media/meia, salud/saude, arena/area)
- **e = ei** (crucero/cruceiro)
- **ue = o** (puerta/porta, puerta/porta)
- **j = x** (junta/xunta, Jesús/Xesús)

Plurals of abbreviations: the letters are doubled
(for example, FF.CC, ferrocarriles – seen on road signs crossing railway tracks)

Words beginning with al-, a- are usually of Arabic origin
(for example, azúcar, alcalde, algodón, albericoque, almacén, almohada).

For those pilgrims who like to attend mass and would like to be able to participate at least once during the service, the text of the Lord's Prayer is given here in Spanish:

> *Padre nuestro, que estás en el cielo,*
> *santificado sea tu Nombre;*
> *venga a nosotros tu reino;*
> *hágase tu voluntad en la tierra como en el cielo.*
> *Danos hoy nuestra pan de cada día;*
> *perdona nuestras ofensas,*
> *como también nosotros perdonamos*
> *a los que nos ofenden;*
> *no nos dejes caer en la tentación,*
> *y líbranos del mal.*

APPENDIX F
Index of Maps

APPENDIX G
Summary of Route

APPENDIX H
Index of Principal Place Names

LISTING OF CICERONE GUIDES

- THE ISLE OF SKYE – A WALKER'S GUIDE
- WALKS IN THE LAMMERMUIRS
- WALKING IN THE LOWTHER HILLS
- THE SCOTTISH GLENS SERIES
  1 – CAIRNGORM GLENS
  2 – ATHOLL GLENS
  3 – GLENS OF RANNOCH
  4 – GLENS OF TROSSACH
  5 – GLENS OF ARGYLL
  6 – THE GREAT GLEN
  7 – THE ANGUS GLENS
  8 – KNOYDART TO MORVERN
  9 – THE GLENS OF ROSS-SHIRE
- SCOTTISH RAILWAY WALKS
- SCRAMBLES IN LOCHABER
- SCRAMBLES IN SKYE
- SKI TOURING IN SCOTLAND
- THE SPEYSIDE WAY
- TORRIDON – A WALKER'S GUIDE
- WALKS FROM THE WEST HIGHLAND RAILWAY
- THE WEST HIGHLAND WAY
- WINTER CLIMBS NEVIS & GLENCOE

IRELAND
- IRISH COASTAL WALKS
- THE IRISH COAST TO COAST
- THE MOUNTAINS OF IRELAND

WALKING AND TREKKING IN THE ALPS
- WALKING IN THE ALPS
- 100 HUT WALKS IN THE ALPS
- CHAMONIX TO ZERMATT
- GRAND TOUR OF MONTE ROSA VOL. 1 AND VOL. 2
- TOUR OF MONT BLANC

FRANCE, BELGIUM AND LUXEMBOURG
- WALKING IN THE ARDENNES
- ROCK CLIMBS BELGIUM & LUX.
- THE BRITTANY COASTAL PATH
- CHAMONIX - MONT BLANC WALKING GUIDE
- WALKING IN THE CEVENNES
- CORSICAN HIGH LEVEL ROUTE: GR20
- THE ECRINS NATIONAL PARK
- WALKING THE FRENCH ALPS: GR5
- WALKING IN THE FRENCH GORGES
- FRENCH ROCK
- WALKING IN THE HAUTE SAVOIE
- WALKING IN THE LANGUEDOC
- TOUR OF THE OISANS: GR54
- WALKING IN PROVENCE
- THE PYRENEAN TRAIL: GR10
- THE TOUR OF THE QUEYRAS
- ROBERT LOUIS STEVENSON TRAIL
- WALKING IN TARENTAISE & BEAUFORTAIN ALPS
- ROCK CLIMBS IN THE VERDON
- TOUR OF THE VANOISE
- WALKS IN VOLCANO COUNTRY
- SNOWSHOEING MONT BLANC/WESTERN ALPS
- VANOISE SKI TOURING
- ALPINE SKI MOUNTAINEERING
  VOL 1: WESTERN ALPS
  VOL 2: EASTERN ALPS

FRANCE/SPAIN
- ROCK CLIMBS IN THE PYRENEES

- WALKS & CLIMBS IN THE PYRENEES
- THE WAY OF ST JAMES VOL 1 AND VOL 2 – WALKER'S
- THE WAY OF ST JAMES LE PUY TO SANTIAGO – CYCLIST'S

SPAIN AND PORTUGAL
- WALKING IN THE ALGARVE
- ANDALUSIAN ROCK CLIMBS
- BIRDWATCHING IN MALLORCA
- COSTA BLANCA ROCK
- COSTA BLANCA WALKS VOL 1
- COSTA BLANCA WALKS VOL 2
- WALKING IN MALLORCA
- ROCK CLIMBS IN MAJORCA, IBIZA & TENERIFE
- WALKING IN MADEIRA
- THE MOUNTAINS OF CENTRAL SPAIN
- THE SPANISH PYRENEES GR11 2ND EDITION
- WALKING IN THE SIERRA NEVADA
- WALKS & CLIMBS IN THE PICOS DE EUROPA
- VIA DE LA PLATA
- WALKING IN THE CANARY ISLANDS VOL 1: WEST AND VOL 2: EAST

SWITZERLAND
- ALPINE PASS ROUTE, SWITZERLAND
- THE BERNESE ALPS A WALKING GUIDE
- CENTRAL SWITZERLAND
- THE JURA: HIGH ROUTE & SKI TRAVERSES
- WALKING IN TICINO, SWITZERLAND
- THE VALAIS, SWITZERLAND – A WALKING GUIDE

GERMANY, AUSTRIA AND EASTERN EUROPE
- MOUNTAIN WALKING IN AUSTRIA
- WALKING IN THE BAVARIAN ALPS
- WALKING IN THE BLACK FOREST
- THE DANUBE CYCLE WAY
- GERMANY'S ROMANTIC ROAD
- WALKING IN THE HARZ MOUNTAINS
- KING LUDWIG WAY
- KLETTERSTEIG NORTHERN LIMESTONE ALPS
- WALKING THE RIVER RHINE TRAIL
- THE MOUNTAINS OF ROMANIA
- WALKING IN THE SALZKAMMERGUT
- HUT-TO-HUT IN THE STUBAI ALPS
- THE HIGH TATRAS
- WALKING IN HUNGARY

SCANDINAVIA
- WALKING IN NORWAY
- ST OLAV'S WAY

ITALY AND SLOVENIA
- ALTA VIA – HIGH LEVEL WALKS DOLOMITES
- CENTRAL APENNINES OF ITALY
- WALKING CENTRAL ITALIAN ALPS
- WALKING IN THE DOLOMITES
- SHORTER WALKS IN THE DOLOMITES
- WALKING ITALY'S GRAN PARADISO
- LONG DISTANCE WALKS IN ITALY'S GRAN PARADISO
- ITALIAN ROCK
- WALKS IN THE JULIAN ALPS
- WALKING IN SICILY

- WALKING IN TUSCANY
- VIA FERRATA SCRAMBLES IN THE DOLOMITES
- VIA FERRATAS OF THE ITALIAN DOLOMITES
  VOL 1: NORTH, CENTRAL AND EAST
  VOL 2: SOUTHERN DOLOMITES, BRENTA AND LAKE GARDA

OTHER MEDITERRANEAN COUNTRIES
- THE ATLAS MOUNTAINS
- WALKING IN CYPRUS
- CRETE – THE WHITE MOUNTAINS
- THE MOUNTAINS OF GREECE
- JORDAN – WALKS, TREKS, CAVES ETC.
- THE MOUNTAINS OF TURKEY
- TREKS & CLIMBS WADI RUM JORDAN
- CLIMBS & TREKS IN THE ALA DAG
- WALKING IN PALESTINE

HIMALAYA
- ADVENTURE TREKS IN NEPAL
- ANNAPURNA – A TREKKER'S GUIDE
- EVEREST – A TREKKERS' GUIDE
- GARHWAL & KUMAON – A TREKKER'S GUIDE
- KANGCHENJUNGA – A TREKKER'S GUIDE
- LANGTANG, GOSAINKUND & HELAMBU TREKKERS GUIDE
- MANASLU – A TREKKER'S GUIDE

OTHER COUNTRIES
- MOUNTAIN WALKING IN AFRICA – KENYA
- OZ ROCK – AUSTRALIAN CRAGS
- WALKING IN BRITISH COLUMBIA
- TREKKING IN THE CAUCASUS
- GRAND CANYON & AMERICAN SOUTH WEST
- ROCK CLIMBS IN HONG KONG
- ADVENTURE TREKS WEST NORTH AMERICA
- CLASSIC TRAMPS IN NEW ZEALAND

TECHNIQUES AND EDUCATION
- OUTDOOR PHOTOGRAPHY
- SNOW & ICE TECHNIQUES
- ROPE TECHNIQUES
- THE BOOK OF THE BIVVY
- THE HILLWALKER'S MANUAL
- THE TREKKER'S HANDBOOK
- THE ADVENTURE ALTERNATIVE
- BEYOND ADVENTURE
- FAR HORIZONS – ADVENTURE TRAVEL FOR ALL
- MOUNTAIN WEATHER

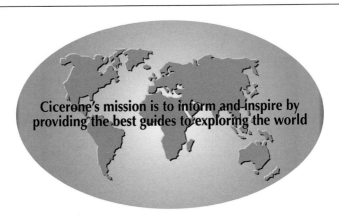

Cicerone's mission is to inform and inspire by
providing the best guides to exploring the world

Since its foundation over 30 years ago, Cicerone has specialised in
publishing guidebooks and has built a reputation for quality and reliability.
It now publishes nearly 300 guides to the major destinations for outdoor
enthusiasts, including Europe, UK and the rest of the world.

Written by leading and committed specialists, Cicerone guides are
recognised as the most authoritative. They are full of information, maps and
illustrations so that the user can plan and complete a successful and safe
trip or expedition – be it a long face climb, a walk over Lakeland fells, an
alpine traverse, a Himalayan trek or a ramble in the countryside.

With a thorough introduction to assist planning, clear diagrams, maps and
colour photographs to illustrate the terrain and route, and accurate and
detailed text, Cicerone guides are designed for ease of use and access to
the information.

If the facts on the ground change, or there is any aspect of a guide that you
think we can improve, we are always delighted to hear from you.

Cicerone Press
2 Police Square Milnthorpe Cumbria LA7 7PY
Tel:01539 562 069   Fax:01539 563 417
e-mail:info@cicerone.co.uk   web:www.cicerone.co.uk